PROFESSIONAL DEVELOPMENT AND PRACTICE SERIES

Ann Lieberman, Editor

Editorial advisory board: Myrna Cooper, Nathalie Gehrke,
Gary Griffin, Judith Warren Little, Lynne Miller,
Phillip Schlechty, Gary Sykes

Building a Professional Culture in Schools
Ann Lieberman, editor

The Contexts of Teaching in Secondary Schools:
Teachers' Realities
*Milbrey W. McLaughlin, Joan E. Talbert,
and Nina Bascia, editors*

Careers in the Classroom:
When Teaching Is More Than a Job
Sylvia Mei-ling Yee

CAREERS IN THE CLASSROOM

When Teaching Is More Than a Job

Sylvia Mei-ling Yee

Teachers College, Columbia University
New York and London

To a talented and dedicated teacher,
my mother, Nancy Wong Yee.

Published by Teachers College Press, 1234 Amsterdam Avenue,
New York, NY 10027

Library of Congress Cataloging-in-Publication Data

Yee, Sylvia Mei-ling.
    Careers in the classroom : when teaching is more than a job /
Sylvia Mei-ling Yee.
        p.   cm. — (Professional development and practice series)
    Includes bibliographical references (p.   ).
    ISBN 0-8077-3038-6 (alk. paper). — ISBN 0-8077-3037-8 (pbk. :
alk. paper)
    1. High school teachers — United States.   2. High school teachers —
United States — Case studies.   3. Teacher turnover — United States —
Case studies.   4. Teaching satisfaction — Case studies.
5. Teachers — United States — Interviews.   I. Title.   II. Series.
LB1737.U6Y44   1990
373.11'00973 — dc20   90-35706
                                                              CIP

ISBN 0-8077-3038-6 (cloth)
ISBN 0-8077-3037-8 (paper)

Printed on acid-free paper

Manufactured in the United States of America

97 96 95 94 93 92 91 90 8 7 6 5 4 3 2 1

Contents

Foreword

When we began the Professional Development and Practice Series, our intention was to provide a forum for innovative approaches and groundbreaking research in education. In this latest volume of the series, Sylvia Yee ably fulfills that purpose, for the research she reports here demands that we rethink our conception and understanding of a career in teaching.

Up until now, careers have been described primarily in terms of pay, status, job security, and other organizational rewards. While easy to measure and describe, these extrinsic factors are essentially static, and analyses based on them necessarily ignore the social and personal variables that more often are the real determinants of teacher satisfaction and commitment.

Previous volumes in this series have addressed that deficiency by focusing on the school as a cultural milieu and as the context within which teachers work. Sylvia Yee's research builds on these efforts by utilizing a career perspective and by studying individual-level factors. Through her work she has uncovered a whole new set of dynamic connections between teachers' sense of efficacy and competence, on the one hand, and their commitment to and satisfaction with teaching, on the other.

Yee's descriptions of teachers' social construction of satisfaction in the workplace reveal that quality of colleagueship and bonding within the school can differentiate teachers who stay in teaching and continue to work hard in pursuit of student learning from those who do not. Some of the latter leave teaching altogether, while others stay in the field but find insufficient support in the school culture and the intrinsic and extrinsic rewards of teaching to develop and maintain a real connection to the professional life that other teachers enjoy. Yee also examines personal factors (e.g., gender, stage in the life cycle, and initial impetus to enter teaching) and institutional variables (administrative context, opportunity for professional development and advancement) that profoundly affect commitment, job satisfaction, and performance but are often neglected as important variables.

Unlike existing research, Yee's work incorporates interviews with former teachers along with survey and interview data from present teachers. The examples in her book of how factors interact and play out in actual teachers' lives therefore cover the entire range of career outcomes. Moreover, by conducting her research in three very different school settings — an inner city, a wealthy suburb, and a working-class area — Yee has been able to gather information about the causes of the uneven distribution of attrition that often challenges conventional assumptions.

Major themes that emerge from the cases of individual teachers in these schools are critically important to an enhanced understanding of a teacher's career, especially at a time when half of the teaching force will retire within the next decade. One particularly significant finding is the importance of permitting professional discretion rather than maintaining bureaucratic, top-down control: Teachers want greater input so that they can be more competent in their work, not just to make teaching easier, and they want increased professional development for the same reason. This linkage between a sense of self-efficacy and overall commitment to teaching, and between job satisfaction and intrinsic (rather than extrinsic) rewards, is demonstrated throughout the book as a key factor in career decisions and attitudes. These findings lead to important policy considerations not only for how to motivate teachers to remain in the classroom, but for helping them sustain a commitment to excellence in their profession. Conventional approaches to teacher retention, such as merit pay and career ladders, are called into question when we properly understand the real basis of teachers' career satisfaction: continuous opportunity to grow, learn, and become more expert in their work. Such a message is both timely and significant. Let us hope it is heeded.

Ann Lieberman
Series Editor

Preface

Who is going to teach tomorrow's students? The answer to this question is a major concern confronting policy makers as they face teacher shortages and search for ways to improve public education. The issue is not simply the number of teachers remaining or leaving the profession, but also the kind of teachers that are staying or leaving. Are they the best? The most motivated? The relationship between teacher quality and tenure is critical to understanding both teacher retention and school improvement. The problem is further complicated by serious equity concerns. Inner city schools, with predominantly poor, ethnic minority students, experience higher rates of teacher turnover.

The future quality of schools hinges on who will teach. Yet the recent spate of state-level reform bills has been remarkably uninformed by key players in education reform — classroom teachers. Since teachers' support and participation are essential to school improvement, *Careers in the Classroom* captures teachers' views about the factors that motivate them and keep them committed.

When I began to explore these retention issues, I found that voluntary turnover from the profession within the past five years has been modest. In many school districts, financial cutbacks and declining student enrollments had resulted in layoffs of the less experienced teachers, from whom the bulk of the voluntary exits normally are drawn. This has produced relatively stable, older faculties. The schools included in my study reflect this trend.

This demographic fact of school life shaped my research in fundamental and important ways. It led me to examine not only why teachers leave or stay, but how they develop a sense of career. Consequently, this book moves beyond the traditional approaches to teacher retention in several respects. It illuminates the factors that affect teachers' levels of involvement and job satisfaction as well as the process by which they arrive at their career decisions. The book also explores the diversity of career patterns within the context of sharply contrasting workplaces with varying levels of attrition: an inner-city school in New York;

a wealthy suburban school in the San Francisco Bay Area; and a work-ing-class, suburban school outside of Los Angeles.

The analysis presented here is based on case studies and in-depth interviews conducted in 1986, along with surveys of teachers at the three sites. Talks with site administrators, document inspection, and observations supplement the interviews and surveys. Unlike existing research, this work incorporates interviews with teachers who have actu-ally quit.

Schools are not equal as places in which to teach. The portraits of the three high schools not only dramatize the range in variation of teaching jobs across schools; they highlight the ways in which workplace conditions influence career patterns and how sources of satisfaction and reward vary significantly. The interviews with teachers reveal that the level and direction of teachers' effort and performance are also the result of experiences in the workplace and not simply a product of individual disposition or personality. Positive workplace experiences are crucial to the development of a sense of success that can lead to strong professional involvement.

These findings challenge existing models of career development for teachers and lead to important questions of how to motivate teachers, not only to remain in the classroom but to retain their commitment to excellence in teaching. They also raise doubts about conventional solu-tions to teacher retention that rely primarily on such extrinsic rewards as merit pay and career ladders.

Understanding career development for teachers provides a key to how to think about school reform, because whether teachers are able to develop a positive sense of career carries great significance not only for individual teachers but for students and schools as well.

Acknowledgments

A central theme of this book is the importance of supportive work-place conditions to a teacher's sense of career and achievement. This theme is mirrored in my own "career" as a doctoral student at Stanford University, where I was nurtured by a rich network of support. I owe much to my dissertation committee members for their guidance: Joan Talbert for her careful and very detailed feedback and Jim March for pushing me to offer alternative perspectives or explanations.

My advisor, Milbrey McLaughlin, played a key role in my professional growth, taking personal interest not only in my research, but in me. The inspiration for this study came from her work on school change and educational policy, and this book would have been impossible without her close attention and encouragement. I am extremely fortunate to have had her as a mentor and a friend.

Seeing this project through required both financial and moral support. My colleagues and friends gave me vital encouragement, cheering the breakthroughs and insisting that I stay on track. I especially want to mention Annette Lareau, Brian DeLaney, Gretchen Dykstra, and members of my doctoral support group—Jackie Schmidt Posner, Debbie Leong-Childs, Patrick Murphy, Scott Pfeifer, Charles Sullivan, and Anna Waring. I am indebted to Donna Terman of the Walter S. Johnson Foundation for believing in the importance of this study and providing a grant to make travel to the three schools possible. The Walter S. Johnson Foundation also supported an earlier piece of research on the sources of teacher satisfaction and effectiveness that laid the groundwork for this book. Of course, *Careers in the Classroom* reflects my views and not necessarily those of the Foundation. I am also grateful to Dave Florio, formerly with the American Federation of Teachers, for his enthusiastic encouragement to pursue this topic.

My husband, Brian McCaffrey, was a real partner in this effort— as he is in my life—editing the many drafts, providing babysitting on evenings and weekends, and maintaining a sense a of balance during the inevitable dry periods of the writing process.

Finally, this study could not have been done without the cooperation and support of the many teachers and administrators in the three study schools. They gave graciously and generously of their time and insights, appreciative that a researcher was interested in what they had to say. Unfortunately, I cannot acknowledge them individually since the personal nature of the research requires that they remain anonymous. My thanks to these individuals, most of whom have committed themselves to careers in the classroom.

CAREERS IN THE CLASSROOM

When Teaching Is More Than a Job

CHAPTER 1

Teacher Retention and Teaching Careers

Will the nation's classrooms have the teachers they need as the next big wave of students enters school? The proportion of young people wanting to be teachers has sharply decreased over the past 15 years. Already shortages of math, science, and bilingual teachers exist in many parts of the country. The problem will only grow worse as a quarter of those already in the teaching force are likely to leave the classroom in the near future (Harris, 1985). The issue before policy makers, however, is not simply the number of teachers remaining and leaving, but who leaves and where they leave from.

Not all teachers are professionally involved and committed, so knowing the kind of teacher who leaves is critical. Efforts to retain all teachers would be counterproductive, since some teachers should be allowed, even encouraged, to leave. Thus understanding why disengaged teachers stay is as important as understanding why committed teachers leave. The dynamic between teacher quality and turnover, however, remains largely unexplored.

Attrition is highest where the need is most acute. Inner-city schools, known for their tough and stressful conditions, generally have the greatest shortages of teachers as well as the highest rates of transfers to other schools and defectors from the profession (Bruno & Doscher, 1981; Dworkin, 1980; Herriott & St. John, 1966). This pattern signals critical equity concerns. Yet the considerable research on inner-city schools has shed little light on how specific workplace contexts affect career decisions.

What *is* known is that high rates of turnover carry serious implications for the quality of education. The so-called effective schools research highlights the importance of staff stability and continuity in successful schools. Frequent turnover inhibits the formation of a productive and coherent school culture (Purkey & Smith, 1983), obstructing the development of shared norms for academic achievement – an essential component of effective schools (Hawley & Rosenholtz, 1984). Why teachers stay at some schools and leave others is of considerable consequence to school managers and policy makers.

1

WORKPLACE CONDITIONS, SATISFACTION, AND RETENTION

Workplace factors contribute to job satisfaction and subsequently to decisions to stay or leave a job by offering organizational inducements or rewards. Researchers looking at employee turnover conclude that workplace conditions (including pay, security, workload, relations with the supervisor) act as inducements for workers to stay (Barnard, 1962; Simon, 1961).

Satisfaction with these inducements is an important gauge of the likelihood of defection. In turnover models (March & Simon, 1958; Mobley, 1982) the greater the organizational rewards in relation to the personal contributions, the greater the satisfaction and the smaller the propensity to leave. Conversely, dissatisfaction may generate the search for job alternatives and make movement from the organization desirable. Satisfaction results from a subjective evaluation of work conditions. The greater the conformity of job characteristics to an individual's needs, self-image, and other roles, the greater the satisfaction (Hackman & Oldham, 1980). To some individuals the fit between teaching hours and family responsibilities may be more significant than the actual teaching work. How satisfaction is constructed must be investigated, and personal factors (other roles, interests, values) should be considered. Looking simply at the level of satisfaction obscures understanding of the personal and complex way that it is arrived at.

Although useful, satisfaction ratings tell only part of the story. Job satisfaction is consistently, although moderately, related to attrition and retention (Mobley, 1982). Correlations are generally less than .40 (Locke, 1976). This loose relationship highlights two things: variables other than job satisfaction influence career decisions, and low job satisfaction may have other consequences in addition to turnover. In other words, a teacher can be committed to remaining in the classroom yet dissatisfied with the job. Alternatively, a teacher can be satisfied with working conditions but minimally involved in teaching. The concept of satisfaction and the turnover models that rely on it are of limited usefulness for understanding the dynamic between teacher quality and retention.

Since most turnover studies consider organizational rather than occupational attrition, they fail to distinguish between job site factors (workload, relations with administration, opportunities for professional growth) and occupational factors (the structure of benefits—e.g., job security, hours, vacations). This is pertinent to why teachers may leave the profession, not merely transfer to another school or district. This distinction between characteristics that are part of the occupation and those unique to the job site allows inspection of the interaction between the two factors.

TEACHER MOTIVATION AND QUALITY

Research on reward structures in public schools suggests differences between motivational patterns of professional and production-oriented organizations (Spuck, 1974). Many people are drawn to teaching by a strong service ethic or strong client orientation. The norms of the teaching profession are such that teachers attribute greater importance to intrinsic reward — the psychic, intangible benefits from making a difference in the classroom (Johnson, 1986; Lortie, 1975; McLaughlin, Pfeifer, Swanson-Owens, & Yee, 1986). This perspective indicates that extrinsic rewards such as pay and promotion, which typically are emphasized in turnover research, would have a qualified or limited effect on teachers' decisions to stay. Indeed, teachers view merit pay and career ladder schemes with skepticism (Freiberg, 1984; Johnson, 1986). Exploring how teachers weigh extrinsic and intrinsic rewards in making career decisions would greatly inform policy makers' efforts to make the teaching profession more attractive.

Research on teacher effectiveness raises other factors ignored in studies of attrition but central to the investigation of the relationship between teacher longevity and quality. The quality of teachers' performance in the classroom is only partially due to academic capacity, an indicator that many studies rely on for their conclusions about the declining quality of teachers (Schlechty & Vance, 1981, 1983). Excellent teaching requires many skills: interpersonal, group management, and organizational. Many are not conducive to evaluation by standardized tests (Darling-Hammond, Wise, & Pease, 1983). How then can teacher quality be understood?

The teacher effectiveness literature emphasizes several teacher characteristics that are related to classroom effectiveness and offer more sensitive criteria of quality than academic ability. Effort — the time, energy, and enthusiasm teachers expend on their work — can make a difference between excellent and mediocre teaching, between the willingness to go above and beyond what is minimally required and just getting by (Ashton & Webb, 1986; Macrorie, 1984; McLaughlin & Marsh, 1978). A sense of efficacy — teachers' belief that they make a difference with students — is another characteristic found to be related to high classroom performance (Ashton & Webb, 1986; Berman &

McLaughlin, 1978; McLaughlin & Marsh, 1978). Teachers with a high
sense of efficacy believe that their actions and effort personally contribute to student achievement — teachers' major source of intrinsic reward
and job satisfaction. This suggests a close link between perceived self-
efficacy, classroom effectiveness, and job satisfaction.

Self-efficacy and effort, jointly referred to as "professional involvement," are indicators of teacher effectiveness and permit inspection of
the relationship of teacher quality to career choices.

Unique elements for understanding teacher retention emerge from
the research on teacher and school effectiveness: the value of intrinsic
versus extrinsic rewards for teachers and the relationship of professional
involvement to teacher effectiveness and job satisfaction.

PROFESSIONAL INVOLVEMENT AND
WORKPLACE CONDITIONS

If a sense of efficacy and competence is related to teachers' commitment and satisfaction, how is this sense developed? Professional socialization and identification, although not generally associated in the literature with the work on retention and attrition, also influence teacher
quality and longevity. Professional identification implies attachment to
goals and values as well as active effort; the object of loyalty is the
occupation, not the employing organization — a point pertinent to why
teachers stay in the profession.

Socialization experiences and development of competence through
training and interaction with colleagues are pivotal to the notion of
bonding to a profession (Becker & Carper, 1966). The literature on
professional development in teaching highlights the strong role that
collegial exchange and collaboration play in successful schools (Little,
1982). This raises the issue of organizational support for the development of professional competence and argues for examination of additional factors, such as early training, collegial exchange, feedback, and
opportunities for growth (Berlew & Hall, 1977; Chapman, 1984; Hall &
Schneider, 1973; Schein, 1977). Socialization also implies that the formation of professional competence and bonding (the commitment to
stay) is the result of an evolutionary and dynamic process.

In contrast, traditional turnover studies treat retention as a static
phenomenon; they rely heavily on sources of immediate dissatisfaction
and attraction and neglect contextual or earlier influences related to the
development of professional efficacy and identification.

Administrative context — the degree to which employees are empowered with discretion and influence in a workplace — is a condition that influences a teacher's involvement, satisfaction, and sense of efficacy (Hackman & Oldham, 1980; Kanter, 1983; Newman, Rutter, & Smith, 1985). The chronic tension between bureaucratic and professional control constitutes a classic theme in the literature on professionals in organizations (Etzioni, 1969; Ritzer, 1977; Scott, 1966, 1981) and in research on schools (Cox & Wood, 1980; Metz, 1986).

According to researchers on school context (McNeil, 1986), schools organized around hierarchical, bureaucratic control deprive teachers of meaningful input and consequently are often places where both teachers and students regard education less seriously, resulting in low involvement and effort.

Workplaces providing opportunities for growth tend to produce effective, highly involved teachers. These schools allow teachers to develop increasing degrees of professional competence and provide organizational arrangements that empower staff by allowing discretion and influence in work conditions.

Although the importance of opportunities for growth to individual motivation and performance is recognized in the job redesign and organizational behavior literature (Hackman & Oldham, 1980; Kanter, 1983), discussions of the professional concerns of teachers are notably absent in the usual turnover models, limiting their ability to deal with the multidimensional problem of teacher retention.

TEACHERS' PERSPECTIVES AND INDIVIDUAL-LEVEL FACTORS

In general, attrition studies of teachers neither capture individual viewpoints nor integrate into their analyses individual aspirations and goals or more enduring orientations toward the occupation. For example, many people who enter teaching do not expect to make it their lifelong career (Mason, Dressel, & Bain, 1959). Teachers often resign after only a few years in the classroom. Schlechty and Vance (1981) estimate that 50% of all teachers leave by the seventh to ninth year. Other studies indicate even higher rates of attrition within the first 5 years (Charters, 1965; Talbert, 1986).

Gender and stage in the life cycle also influence mobility patterns in teaching (Charters, 1976). Women often interrupt their teaching to raise a family and return when the children are grown; men may leave for more lucrative occupations as family responsibilities increase. Values, outside interests, and age are other relevant individual-level characteristics that shape teachers' career choices.

Workplace and individual factors are both theoretically relevant to career construction, although much of the empirical work does not examine these dimensions together (Mowday, Porter, & Steers, 1982).

TEACHING CAREERS

The traditional retention models limit understanding of the problem of teacher retention in several major ways: they avoid the issue of quality and generally fail to take into account differences in performance; they stress extrinsic rewards rather than the intrinsic rewards that teachers value; and they treat the decision to stay or leave as a static event rather than as a result of a dynamic process that evolves over time, as the professional socialization literature suggests.

Situating the problem of attrition and retention within the larger frame of internally defined careers provides a richer, more complete way of approaching the problem. The notion of career has traditionally been framed in largely external or institutional terms of vertical mobility: advancement through a series of hierarchical positions (Slocum, 1966). This formulation prompts some to conclude that teaching is a careerless, dead-end, or flat occupation because so few opportunities for advancement exist (Geer, 1966; Lortie, 1975). In this analysis, ambitious teachers have nowhere to go except out of the profession or into administration, where positions are limited.

Current perspectives, however, no longer dictate that careers involve upward progression through an organizational hierarchy (Louis, 1980). An alternative view is that of careers that are individually rather than externally based. In contrast to the traditional view, this subjective concept of career relies on an internally defined sense of progression and satisfaction (Hughes, 1937; Schein, 1978; Stebbins, 1970; Van Maanen & Barley, 1984).

Recent exploratory research suggests that teachers themselves conceive of career in largely subjective terms rather than in the prevailing bureaucratic sense (Biklen, 1986; McLaughlin & Yee, 1988; Yee, 1986). Career advancement is framed in terms of an ongoing process of professional growth rather than as promotion up a job ladder. Career success is interpreted as making a difference in the classroom.

The notion of career connotes a patterned path taken by an individual across time and space, but what is most significant is the meaning the individual ascribes to that path (Ball & Goodson, 1985; Schein, 1978; Van Maanen, 1977). A career approach requires an insider's perspective, an understanding of what it means from teachers' perspectives to have a classroom career. This implies considering decisions to stay or leave the profession as the result of an evolutionary, dynamic process over time (Katz, 1982; Unruh, 1979), in contrast to the conventional static models. A process-oriented view captures important contextual elements relevant to this inquiry — professional development and personal factors, for example.

Many studies treat turnover/retention simply as a dichotomous variable (those who leave versus those who stay), but this approach masks variation in career outcomes among those still in teaching. Several surveys (Educational Research Service, 1985; Harris, 1985) indicate that of those teachers still in the profession, some report they are likely to leave in the near future, some are uncertain what they want to do, while others state that they are likely to remain in the profession.

A career perspective is more useful, since it treats turnover as one of several outcomes and permits a more accurate, differentiated portrayal of teacher attitudes and behavior. Important questions that emerge are:

- How are individual career choices and attitudes constructed in the workplace?
- How do teachers decide if they will stay in or leave teaching?
- What affects their level of satisfaction and involvement in their work?

STRUCTURE OF THIS STUDY

Case studies and in-depth interviews of individual teachers facilitate the study of teachers' careers in their real-life contexts, providing an interpretive framework in which to consider these pertinent questions. I examined career outcomes from the perspectives of teachers in three comprehensive high schools in which variation in workplace conditions might be expected. Each is considered a "good" school to teach in relative to others in the same district. All are located in metropolitan areas:

Brown, an inner-city school in New York City with a high dropout rate

Rolling Hills, a wealthy suburban school in the San Francisco Bay Area with a large proportion of students going on to four-year colleges

Roosevelt, a working-class, suburban school outside Los Angeles whose students achieve within an average range on standardized tests.

I conducted interviews with 15 former and 44 current teachers.* I specifically included former teachers because few studies include the views of people who have actually left. Respondents represent a range in terms of career stage, age, gender, and subject taught. These interviews with teachers were supplemented by talks with site administrators (principals, assistant principals, and department heads), document inspection, and observations — independent sources of data providing alternative perspectives to the information that teachers offer (see Appendix A, "Teacher Interview Questions"). Site administrators rated teachers' classroom performance to complement self-reports by teachers; school administrators also served as a source of information on workplace arrangements and context.

In addition to interviews, responses from closed-ended surveys of teachers at the three sites were also incorporated (see Appendix B, "Teacher Career Commitment Survey"). A total of 215 teachers completed the written surveys. The response rates were: 64% at Brown High School; 71% at Rolling Hills; and 69% at Roosevelt.

The demographics of the study sample generally reflect those of the national teaching force. Due to the declining enrollments and shrinking financial resources of the past decade, particularly in the metropolitan areas where the three sites are located, districts have been able to hire few new teachers. Therefore fewer than 5% of my survey respondents are between the ages of 21 and 29. This is somewhat less than the 10% in that age category reported nationwide (National Education Association, 1987). On the other hand, 22% of my respondents are over 50 years old, closely corresponding to the percentages reported in the national samples. This figure foreshadows the dramatic number of exits due to retirements in the next 5 years.

This older age structure of the teaching population holds implications for the study of teaching careers. Recall that most turnover occurs within the first 5 to 8 years of teaching. However, this early turnover pattern is not well represented here because it includes so few young teachers. Rather, the career decisions of veteran teachers who have survived the difficult early years occupy center stage. The study focuses on a stable sample relative to schools with younger faculty.

---

*The names of the schools and teachers have been altered to protect the identity of individuals. Some characteristics of teachers judged to be extraneous to the focus of the study were changed to prevent identification.

SCHOOL CONTEXT AND TEACHING CAREERS

The major themes and issues that emerge from the 59 interviews with teachers are illustrated through vignettes of 21 teachers chosen to illustrate the larger sample. These 21 individuals from the three high schools represent diversity in age, gender, principals' evaluation, and career outcomes. The vignettes underscore the complexity of reasons, constructed over the course of a teacher's career, that contribute to professional involvement and commitment to stay in or to leave teaching.

Initial career attitudes or one's predisposition toward teaching are a useful benchmark when examining later career choice and the decision to stay in or leave teaching. Incorporating these individual-level factors into a view of career choice generates career patterns formed by grouping teachers along two individual dimensions: initial career attitudes and current career choice. This grouping allows exploration of how initial attitudes and commitment may be either reinforced or transformed through experiences in the workplace.

Initial career attitudes are measured by teachers' reasons for entering teaching, which fall into two broad categories: good-fit and weak-fit. "Good-fit" teachers are those who entered the profession because of a positive attraction to teaching—for example, a desire to work with young people, a commitment to service, an interest in teaching a particular subject, or inspiration from former teachers. When they entered the profession, many of the good-fit teachers had known for many years that they wanted to become teachers and intended to stay in the profession for a long time. Although it would be easy to conclude that current career choices and attitudes for this group of teachers flow primarily from strong initial commitment to teaching, analysis of their vignettes suggest otherwise.

By contrast, "weak-fit" teachers are those who entered the profession because of a more casual attraction to teaching. Teachers in this category often ended up in teaching by accident or perceived few if any job alternatives to teaching. While good-fit teachers actively chose teaching, weak-fit teachers approached teaching more passively, often saying that they had fallen into teaching or had chosen it by default. Many weak-fit teachers viewed teaching as a temporary job, intending to stay for just a few years. However, many of these teachers evolved into stayers, anticipating that they would remain in the classroom until retirement.

When teachers are grouped by initial and current career attitudes, the resultant career patterns are: good-fit stayers, good-fit undecideds, good-fit leavers, weak-fit stayers, and weak-fit leavers. Although weak-fit undecideds did exist as a category, they are excluded because they contributed little to the analysis as a group.

In the next chapters, portraits of the three schools offer insights into how workplace conditions affect variation in career outcomes. Following each portrait, vignettes of teachers' careers demonstrate how individuals arrive at their career decisions and attitudes within the specific school contexts.

CHAPTER 2

Teaching in the Inner City:
Brown High School

Brown High School is a place of contrasts and contradictions — both a good and a terrible place to teach. Students ride the subway from Harlem to the school, situated on a border between high rise public housing and a newly gentrified area of fashionable boutiques and restaurants serving sushi, pasta, and paté. One of the perquisites of teaching at Brown is the opportunity to eat at a pleasant sidewalk café or to shop at lunch time. As inner-city schools go, this is a relatively good one to teach in. Brown has the reputation of a stable and capable faculty; teachers in other comprehensive schools in the district would welcome the opportunity to work there.

Horace Anderson — a feisty and dedicated man — has been the principal here for over a quarter of a century, a seasoned survivor of district politics, community upheavals, and strong union activity. The faculty is divided in its evaluation of him. Some teachers say they hold great respect, if not affection, for him and for the tough job that he holds. Other faculty members dislike him for being bureaucratic, inflexible, and arbitrary. He frequently locks horns with the teachers' union, which has filed numerous grievances against him. Most teachers will agree, however, that Horace Anderson runs a tight ship. He insists that the walls and floors be kept spotless, and indeed, neither graffiti nor a single wad of paper can be seen.

More significant than this superficial order is the absence of rowdiness or violence. During class time the halls are clear of loitering students. Teachers are able to conduct lessons with their doors open. A middle-aged English teacher spoke of her relief in feeling safe enough to teach without locking her classroom door. Other inner-city schools in the district are not as fortunate. A young teacher related how she lost seven pounds in a single month while teaching at another inner-city school the year before because the environment was "so chaotic." She welcomed the "organization" and order at Brown. When surveyed,

11

nearly three-fourths of the faculty concurred by expressing satisfaction
with the support for discipline in the school.

Compared with colleagues in other inner-city schools, teachers at
Brown are fortunate in another sense. Drugs have not emerged as a
school problem, at least not yet. Elsewhere in the district, the use of
crack cocaine is serious enough that the central administration shows an
educational video to all teachers at the opening of the school year to
help them identify the symptoms of crack use. No one has seen drug
deals in the closely monitored hallways or cafeteria at Brown, but teachers are concerned about the potential problem on campus. A black
teacher, probably mistaken for a student or resident of the public housing nearby, reported being offered some crack for sale within a block of
school. A white teacher in her fifties also complained that despite her
general oblivion to street activity she recently witnessed two sales just
around the corner from the school's front door.

Brown's vulnerability to the outside world is evidenced by the elab-
orate system of security at the school, a five-storied building occupying
a city block. Students enter and exit by only one door. Upon arrival,
they slide plastic identification cards through a machine that registers
daily attendance. At the front door, uniformed security staff, equipped
with walkie-talkies, question visitors and require them to sign their
names and destinations. Other doors in the building are guarded to
prevent unauthorized passage.

These measures protect the school from intrusion. This electronic
attendance process will also eventually do away with homerooms, a
situation many teachers welcome because it will eliminate some bureaucratic tasks. Other teachers, however, regret the upcoming reform,
since homeroom is the only time they are free to socialize with and give
personal attention to students.

Despite the impressive institutional order, however, the school is not
an easy place to work or to have a satisfying career.

COMMUNITY CHARACTERISTICS:
STUDENT COMPOSITION AND ACHIEVEMENT

The student body is 98% black and Hispanic, a stark contrast to the
overwhelmingly white faculty (92%) and administration, most of whom
commute from the suburbs into the city. Many students speak a language other than English in the home; about 400 of them are enrolled in
bilingual or English-as-a-second-language courses. Language barriers
and the distance between the homes and the school preclude close ties

between teachers and parents. Consequently, 80% of the faculty feel that parent support is inadequate.

Over half of the students qualify for a free lunch or some other form of state aid. In the 1970s Brown High School occupied two campuses, offering triple sessions to serve more than 7,000 students. With declining enrollment, the school has settled back into one building—a relief to the faculty who had to trek between the two sites. School year 1985–86 was the first time in 24 years that Brown had a normal eight-period day. They began the year with about 3,000 students, but by May had lost 600 to 700, many of whom are difficult to locate. Only 20% of a recent ninth-grade class made it through the twelfth grade at Brown. Over half of the ninth graders never graduate from any high school. Brown receives a large state grant to address this serious problem of student attrition.

Surprisingly, of the minority who survive through the twelfth grade (a total of 381 graduates in 1986), about three-quarters enter four-year colleges. A handful are courted by the best colleges. However, most of the graduates are accepted into college through open or special admissions programs, which make allowances for the students' educational and economic disadvantage. A social studies teacher noted dejectedly:

> Students are guaranteed admission to college. I was a college advisor for a year, and the dropout rate after the first year in college is very high—precisely from students like ours. Most know our kids are not capable of dealing with college work. They are reading two years behind grade level. Our kids take tests over and over [to try to pass competency tests]. The bottom line is that most can't read an article in the *New York Times*.

Results from the Regents Exam, a statewide testing program, support teachers' assessments of the intensity and diversity of student needs. Only half of the seniors take these exams; of those who participate, only 40% pass. Table 2.1 summarizes major characteristics of Brown High School.

WORKLOAD AND SOURCES OF STRESS

Steve Philips, an outstanding teacher according to Horace Anderson's evaluation, spends more than 60 hours a week on his social studies teaching. The contractual class size is 34 students. With student attri-

TABLE 2.1. Summary of School Characteristics, Brown High School

Location: New York City
Grades: 9-12
Number of teachers employed full time: 150
Average class size: 33
Number of students enrolled in September 1986: 3,000
Ethnicity of students: 99% Hispanic & black; 1% white
Ethnicity of faculty: 92% white
Student socioeconomic status: Poor & working class; 50% qualify for
                                                         state welfare
Daily student absences: 16-18%
Dropout rate: 50%-60% of 9th graders

tion, his actual class size is about 30. He explained how this affects his work:

> The [class] size is unrealistic. Two-thirds of our students are two or more levels below grade. Their self-image is extremely low. They need individual attention. For example, they need teachers who will read what they write. We have 150 to 175 students each. A few of us are crazy to give writing assignments every night. . . . We have set up a system of failure. Teachers who care the most feel it deeply.

An articulate and expressive woman, Marilyn Moore has been teaching English for 17 years. She is tired and wants out. She can appreciate things at Brown that help her do her best in the classroom — for example, "the good security in keeping intruders out," free breakfast and lunch for students, innovative programs like Poets in the Schools, and having an appreciative department chair. But these are not enough for Marilyn. Central to her dissatisfaction is the impossibility of the task and her inability to do the job right. Marilyn described her efforts as "fighting a losing battle":

> Teaching takes so much out of me, having five classes a day. It's extraordinarily difficult work. The worst thing for me is the number of kids and the number of other cultures they come from. This leads to the breakdown in discipline. There are more cultural differences between students and teachers, which lead to misunderstandings. Teachers have to be social engineers and get along with kids that even the police can't

deal with. If the classes were smaller — between 18 and 25 — it would be easier.

Class size is not the only issue affecting a teacher's workload and sense of efficacy. Although the school has a specially funded laboratory filled with IBM computers, regular classroom teachers often complain of insufficient materials, especially those appropriate for the low reading levels of their students. In fact, 40% of the faculty rated their classroom materials as "inadequate." Marilyn added that this situation is compounded by a scarcity of planning time:

> I feel I'm effective — [but only] within the constraints. We need more materials and more time. The curriculum is handed down, but we need time to plan it to the level of the kids and with the books that we have available. Time to plan and develop is not respected. At this school, making the institution work is primary and education is secondary.

Yale Andrews, who left teaching after ten years, testified that he had experienced a similar sense of futility, not primarily because of the lack of discipline or inadequate materials, but because of the poor attendance. Sometimes only half the class was present, so continuity from lesson to lesson was difficult to maintain.

Low motivation also exacerbates the low student attendance. In some classes, students complete their homework as infrequently as 25% of the time.

Large class sizes, large numbers of non-English-speaking and remedial students, diversity of ethnic backgrounds, poor attendance, low student motivation, and high dropout rates characterize what one teacher called "the extraordinarily difficult task" of Brown faculty.

Patterns of teaching assignments reflect the difficulty of the task. Nearly a third of the teachers carry a full load of five classes filled predominantly with students who speak limited English or are at least 3 years below grade level. Half of the faculty teach three to five classes composed predominantly of students with remedial needs. Three-quarters of the teachers were not fortunate enough to have a single college preparatory, honors, or advanced placement class.

Given the variety and intensity of the students' educational needs, few of the Brown faculty are rewarded by feelings of success in their work. Only a third of the teachers feel they have accomplished their instructional goals with more than 60% of their students. And only a quarter of the teachers believe that they were "very successful" in getting their students to learn the previous year. Intrinsic rewards of a job well done thus accrue to only a small percentage of the teachers at Brown.

SPECIAL PROGRAMS AND NEW ROLES:
A SAFETY VALVE SYSTEM?

Classroom work is so stressful that teachers welcome the opportunity to take on additional responsibilities and reduce their course load. Brown offers a myriad of specially funded programs to address the severe and varied educational needs of its students: job training, counseling, remedial courses, dropout prevention, bilingual instruction for 700 Hispanic students, tutorials, reading and computer labs. So many activities go on that teachers complain they often are unaware what is happening in the school.

To staff the potpourri of special programs, about 40% of the 150 teachers teach less than a five-period load each day. Instead, they are given time off to manage these special programs or to counsel in them. Other roles, such as school store advisor, security manager, attendance manager, or special student advisor, also enable teachers to carry fewer than five classes. Most of the teachers welcome the chance to decrease their teaching load. An experienced teacher, assigned to coordinate dropout prevention efforts with local colleges, explained: "We need these [nonteaching roles] so we can do a good job in the classroom. Otherwise we are just too tired [to teach a full load]."

Sam Lake, rated by the principal as "an outstanding science teacher," has been teaching for 20 years. He conducts only three classes a day and manages one of the school's special programs the rest of the time. In 5 years his special position will expire. When asked if he would remain in teaching, he responded: "If I get five classes again, no. The workload would be too much."

Indeed, while only 33% of the faculty who teach a full five periods consider their teaching load "manageable," 66% of those with special positions (and who teach only one to four periods a day) consider their work load manageable. Further, 60% of the five-period teachers spend 50 hours or more on classroom responsibilities, whereas only 39% of the teachers with nonteaching duties work as long. Sam philosophized about the function that nonteaching duties play at Brown: "We need them. They relieve a lot of pressure in the system."

To those not lucky enough to get them — about 60% of the faculty — this system of lateral promotion is viewed as a reward mechanism for the principal's favorites and is a source of resentment. A veteran teacher summed up how many teachers evaluate the differentiated role opportunities: "Those who have them [nonteaching duties] like them — and the principal. Those who don't, resent the fact that their class loads are so high."

In order to limit the power of the principal, the union contract restricts the length of time that a teacher can occupy one of these special positions to 6 years. An active member in the union criticized this system of staffing and the number of nonteaching assignments as "scandalous." She argued that 40 of these 50 positions could be assumed by lower-paid clericals, thus enabling class sizes for all teachers to be dramatically cut.

PROFESSIONAL CONCERNS AND BUREAUCRATIC CONTROLS: RELATIONS WITH THE ADMINISTRATION

Horace Anderson commands the respect of a number of teachers. At the same time, the relationship between the principal and union remains confrontational and charged. Anderson is a strong, top-down administrator. He provides a safe, orderly environment in which to work — a remarkable feat in the context of Brown's inner-city setting. Yet the same bureaucratic control that keeps the engine of the school running fails to engage the commitment and involvement of the faculty — the engineers of the system upon whom responsibility for innovation and improvement rests.

Punching in and out on a time clock, filling out a myriad of forms for bureaucratic purposes, having little input into school decisions — these were complaints of Brown faculty who perceive themselves to be "at the low end of the totem pole," beneath the administration. A highly regarded science teacher voiced frequently expressed resentment about the low status of teachers in the school when he said he feels more "like a worker at the bottom of the pecking order" than a professional.

Michael Wexell, who decided to quit after 12 years, elaborated on the demoralizing effects of the bureaucratic practices and climate:

The actual act of teaching was a small part of the day. There was lots of administrative and bureaucratic superstructure laid over the teaching. We were filling out IBM forms for each student and lessons plans for the substitute if we were sick. From the administrative point of view, I could understand it, but from the teacher's point of view, it was a real burden. It was too much of an institutional atmosphere and too little of a collegial one.

Over half the faculty indicated that completing bureaucratic forms is a significant source of stress.

A highly respected teacher who works more than 60 hours a week complained about the absence of teachers' participation in decision making and argued for more professional treatment:

> Education has to be a concept of shared enterprise. There needs to be more of a sense of respect for teachers, a willingness to share authority, for example, in the curriculum and discipline codes. I've seen numerous people enter as intelligent, effective people and leave the job less than that because of the lack of respect. That's essential to the self-image of the teacher and the ability to do a good job.

The school's evaluation process reinforces the faculty's sense of being more like workers than professionals. One novice teacher referred to it as the "gotcha" approach to evaluation. The principal, who prides himself on visiting every teacher's classroom (about 150 in all) at least once during the year, is the target of complaints that he shows up unannounced, stays only 15 minutes — too short a period to see anything — and gives superficial feedback weeks later.

The emphasis on form rather than content prompted another teacher to conclude that yearly evaluations are primarily of "psychological value to the administration" and are of little value to him or his teaching. Another teacher rated by the principal as "below average" also complained about the evaluation system for its absence of substantive concern for what happens with students in the classroom and for the improvement of teachers.

The frustration with the bureaucracy extends beyond the school site. A teacher who declared "I hate my job" wrote about her sense of frustration due to

> participating in a political charade in which the bureaucracy of the Board of Education, the supervisors, and politicians pretend to care about the children's education, but really don't. If they sincerely did, they would give teachers reasonable class sizes, one room to use, . . . more time, and less commands.

Another Brown teacher summed up the effect of the administrative context on teachers when she wrote:

I love working with the students, but I find this bureaucratic setting devastating. Not only does it destroy or stifle creative teachers, but it also does the same to students.

PROFESSIONAL GROWTH

The sparsity of opportunities for professional development prompted a dedicated math teacher to complain that the school administration "lets us die of boredom." The responsibility for professional growth basically falls on the individual teacher. One teacher complained that all her professional development activities are "outside of the school system." Sighed another excellent teacher: "It's hard to sustain that motivation [for continual professional growth] as an individual."

A few department chairs actively encourage the staff to attend conferences in their academic area or to apply for grants to attend summer seminars. One or two are able to participate in outstanding courses with educators from all over the country. For example, with his department chair's prodding, a teacher applied to and attended a stimulating summer seminar on de Tocqueville that was sponsored by the University of California. For the most part, however, teachers feel opportunities for growth occur too infrequently.

The Board of Education offers a few conferences during the year, but securing substitutes and release time to attend them is difficult. Over half (52%) of the faculty assessed "the opportunities for professional growth and learning" as "inadequate"; less than a third (29%) rated these opportunities as "adequate." Further, only 27% of the faculty reported that the number of professional development activities had increased for them over the years; the rest of the faculty reported no change or a decline in participation.

COLLEGIAL INTERACTION AND
PEER RELATIONS

Each department is housed in one of the corners of the five-storied building, a physical arrangement encouraging little informal interaction among the departments. About a third of the faculty congregate in the teacher's dining room for lunch. Some eat off campus; others have lunch in small department offices that can comfortably accommodate only a handful of teachers. Typically, the building is emptied soon after the last bell.

The psychological climate that results from peer interactions also influences career attitudes. A young black teacher, one of a dozen black and Hispanic teachers among a faculty of 150, cited the racist undertones in his interaction with fellow teachers as a major reason for his preparations to leave teaching:

> I'm fed up with the racism in the system. I have been personally insulted. Teachers denigrate kids' ability based on color, making comments like "I teach like in the sixth grade" or "they [students] are all animals." Student customs are laughed at, and there is lying in history.

The racial tension among the staff is also evident in comments by white faculty. A white former teacher expressed his resentment at the district's affirmative action policies, which he believed blocked his advancement to department chair or a district-level position:

> The other big thing [that bothered me about teaching at Brown] was that teachers don't get promoted on ability. It's on the basis of skin and sex instead, or if you speak Spanish. That grated on me — seeing an administrator who couldn't read or write or speak English.

Other teachers who resigned from Brown recalled wanting to escape from the "constant bitching" and to get away from the "teachers who hate what they do." A new teacher who intends to leave observed that many of the teachers around him seem to be "just putting in their time."

Indeed, a climate or perception of widespread dissatisfaction pervades the campus. When asked to rate the satisfaction of the teachers they spend most of their time with, over half of the Brown faculty indicated that they thought their close colleagues were "dissatisfied."

Relationships among the faculty have improved in the recent years. Time has patched the rifts caused by a bitter strike in the 1970s. But no one would characterize the faculty today as "close-knit." While no recent battle has occurred, the lines are drawn between those who have special, nonteaching duties and those who do not; teachers who support bilingual instruction and those who do not; faculty who like the principal and those who do not.

TEACHING CAREERS AT BROWN HIGH SCHOOL

Recall that Brown High School is considered one of the best inner-city schools in New York and that its student enrollment has declined in the past several years. According to Brown's teachers, the voluntary attrition among teachers at this school is slight compared to that in other inner-city schools. Yet compared to Roosevelt and Rolling Hills, Brown has the highest voluntary turnover projections and the highest level of dissatisfaction among the faculty.

According to Brown's survey results, 18% of the faculty are likely to leave teaching. An additional 15% are uncertain whether they will remain in the profession. However, the largest source of imminent attrition is the retirees, who account for 20% of the teachers. Although not dramatic, Brown's voluntary exit rate is notably higher than that at Rolling Hills and Roosevelt, where only 6% and 12%, respectively, are likely to defect over the next 5 years.

A third of the Brown faculty indicates that they are dissatisfied with teaching. While perhaps not impressive by itself, the proportion is startling in comparison with the two other schools—nearly twice as high as at Roosevelt and five times greater than that at Rolling Hills.

The survey data reveal that of the three schools in this study, Brown has the highest proportion of faculty who entered teaching by accident or by default (due to the lack of other job alternatives) and a lower proportion who initially intended to stay in teaching for a long time. In other words, the inner-city workplace attracted or at least ended up with a greater proportion of weak-fit teachers than the two suburban schools. Conversely, Brown has a relatively small share of good-fit stayers. Table 2.2, which lists the major characteristics of the 18 teachers interviewed, delineates the predominance of weak-fit teachers at Brown.

Given the difficult teaching conditions at Brown, what is puzzling is not so much that teachers resign, but why teachers stay, how they make careers within that context, and what explains why some do find satisfaction with teaching in the inner city. Vignettes of teachers' careers at Brown help unravel these puzzles.

Good-Fit Stayer

Steve Philips: "Teaching is what I want to do with my life." A hardworking, articulate social studies teacher, Steve Philips came to teaching 23 years ago because of a strong commitment to social change and a desire to work with young people. Although many teachers at Brown

TABLE 2.2. Interviewees' Characteristics, Brown High School (*n* = 18)

Name	Age	Years in Teaching	Subject Taught	Hours Worked Weekly	Supervisor Evaluation
GOOD-FIT STAYERS					
Peter Carasco	30	10	Science/Math	50	Average
Steve Philips*	47	23	Social Studies	68	Outstanding
GOOD-FIT UNDECIDEDS					
Larry Jordan*	30	1	English	56	Average
GOOD-FIT LEAVERS					
Michael Wexell†	37	12	Social Studies	40	Above Av.
David Jensen*†	40	18	Science	47	Excellent
WEAK-FIT STAYERS					
Jules Jones	24	1	Math	48	Average
Foster Jackson	38	14	Math	40	Above Av.
Sara Cohn*	45	19	Social Studies	40	Average
Helen Tucker	39	18	E.S.L.	50	Outstanding
Fred Baker*	40	17	Reading	40	Below Av.
Susan Dodd*	45	17	English	42	Outstanding
WEAK-FIT LEAVERS					
Bret Coffman	33	4	Social Studies	37	Average
Kristen Dineson	30	8	Science	43	Average
Marilyn Moore*	47	17	English	48	Average
Sam Lake	44	20	Science	38	Outstanding
Gerald Craig*†	43	18	Math	32	Below Av.
Yale Andrews†	32	10	English	38	Excellent
Sarah Morrison†	35	15	Reading	43	Outstanding

*The interview with this teacher is included as a vignette.

†This teacher has already left the profession.

Note: Teachers who say they will quit teaching before they reach 55 years of age and before qualifying for full retirement benefits are considered leavers; teachers who say they will stay in teaching for 5 years but are not sure after that are considered "undecideds."

are weak-fit teachers, Steve represents a dedicated group of good-fit colleagues who were drawn to teaching primarily because they wanted to contribute to society and to be of service to others. Influenced by progressive parents, Steve was active in the social protest movements of the 1960s and turned to teaching after experiencing the futility of working in the city's welfare department. Married to a teacher who shares his values, he intends to stay in the profession, although he may not stay at the same school due to the many frustrations there: "Teaching is essentially what I want to do with my life. I don't see another job that would accomplish more [of what I want to do]." One of his two main reasons for staying in teaching is the knowledge that what he does in the classroom has social value. The other reason he wants to stay in the classroom is the personal satisfaction he receives from working with students and helping them learn.

. Steve started as a regular substitute with no student teaching or education courses behind him. He was given a tough assignment with three separate preparations and students with what he referred to as "considerable deficits." His first assignment was made easier by a personal bonding with a fine supervisor. She observed Steve about three times during the first term, and as he recalls, "a laundry list could have been written" each time for all the things he failed to do correctly. Instead, she made suggestions that were practical. Their relationship based on mutual respect and affection helped him to grow in confidence and skill as a teacher. Today, both administrators and peers regard his teaching highly. A colleague in another department remarked that teachers like Steve Philips are rare these days; new recruits lack the commitment and academic competence that Steve brings to his work.

In a school in which teachers' complaints about lack of student motivation abound, Steve's classes are a striking exception: his students are attentive, prepared, and active. He is a demanding teacher who cares a great deal when students fail to learn. Steve is one of the few teachers who assigns writing each day to his students, and he is more exceptional in his determination to correct each assignment.

During his years of teaching, Steve spent much time in two job-related activities — getting his doctorate and participating in the teachers' union. Last summer he had a grant to do further research in his field, and he usually participates in summer workshops or conferences. He also encourages colleagues in his department to apply for these summer opportunities. During the school year, professional development offerings are few. And for the opportunities that do exist, release time is difficult to get. Steve complains that staff days usually turn into time for "clerical duties to satisfy bureaucrats." For him, professional growth is an important part of what it means to be a teacher, but it takes place through his own initiative and despite the lack of organizational support for it.

Another source of dissatisfaction for Steve is the absence of what he calls "a meaningful role" for teachers in the school. Active as a union representative, he believes that the school is "too bureaucratic" and that the administration holds "absolute control." Steve argues for "more of a

sense of respect for teachers and a willingness to share authority," particularly in the curriculum and the discipline codes, explaining that, for
him, respect for teachers is "essential to the self-image of the teacher
and the ability to do a good job." His hope is that before retiring, he will
work in a school where the principal is "willing to share" because "education has to be a shared enterprise."

Steve feels that little exists at the school to support his effectiveness
as a teacher—except having the freedom in the classroom to teach the
way he wants. But even that freedom is being eroded. The district
administration has made things "more oppressive" for teachers in their
move to standardize instruction, so that "the same lessons are taught in
the same way with the same exams" throughout all schools. He argues
that this has a detrimental effect on good teaching: "Standardization
does not mean better teaching. Teachers need to teach from individual
strengths and to be creative. That makes them better teachers."

Steve's battles with the principal over school issues such as class size
and his long hours spent in class preparation have made him weary. So
why does he persist in teaching? Teaching allows him to live out his
personal and social values—his progressive vision of the future. Committed to reforming the "system of failure" at Brown, he perseveres as a
teacher and as a union activist to try to make the school a place where
students can learn and teachers can teach.

Good-Fit Undecided

**Larry Jordan: "I like teaching, but if the workload doesn't decrease I
won't continue."** Larry Jordan, who is completing his first year of
teaching, has a contingent attitude toward staying in teaching. He has
just switched from being shop steward in a trucking company to education.

Ten years ago he was interested in teaching because he wanted to
work with young people and to do something that would fit his progressive political ideals, but the tight market for teachers precluded this
from becoming a reality. In the last two years he decided to leave his
former job because of the lack of intellectual stimulation and the low
pay. He heard that teaching positions were opening up again, and that
encouraged him to enroll in the education courses required for a credential. "Teaching is attractive," Larry says, "because I want to be involved
in something intellectually stimulating and with ideas. I like reading."

Now in his early thirties, Larry is starting out as an English teacher
at Brown, but his attitude toward staying in teaching is conditional.
During his first year in the classroom, Larry discovered that teaching at

Brown was not what he had expected the work to be like. He was surprised by the students' absence of basic skills and by how he had to adjust or water down his teaching. Like many other Brown teachers, Larry feels the large class sizes and the intensity of student needs prevent him from reaching the students in the way he should be:

> This school's not what I expected teaching to be like. Students have such poor knowledge. They're like junior high or elementary students. I'm not interested in teaching at the elementary level. The majority of students are so far behind. I water down what they should be doing.
>
> I teach two special classes of kids who are at the third- or fourth-grade level. It's foolish to do the standard curriculum with them. They should just improve their life skills so they can read insurance forms or take the driver's test. Most are not interested in English, and I have to tell them everything and lecture [instead of having discussions].
>
> My other classes go fairly well, considering English is not their first language. They get a decent amount from class. I try to do inferential and critical thinking skills with them.
>
> A lot of kids need smaller classes and individual tutoring. I've got a lot of kids who can't handle the work and become discipline problems.

This year Larry attended graduate courses two evenings a week and, in addition, spent about 56 hours a week on his job. He had so little free time that his relationship with his girlfriend suffered and they decided to separate, leading him to complain: "I take work home every day and do it all the time. I like teaching, but if the workload doesn't decrease, I won't continue." The constant drudgery of correcting papers and the frustration of always being behind are the primary drawbacks of the job. He observes that many of the teachers survive by merely spot-checking the homework that they are required to assign. So far he has not done that.

Other sources of dissatisfaction are the lack of constructive feedback from the administration and the atmosphere of intimidation at Brown:

> The administration is not supportive. They create an environment of intimidation instead of support. The principal observed me once 2 months ago. I don't have a full report from that visit yet. The principal does 10 to 15 observations a day

for 15 to 20 minutes each. This is an ineffective method of evaluation. The principal will come in even on the last day of class to see if you're working. Not many teachers shirk their responsibility, yet he acts as if everybody is trying to put something over him.

Although the workplace is a source of stress and frustration, Larry thinks he may stay in teaching because he does receive satisfaction from his interaction with the students and the subject matter:

I like teaching—being involved with the kids. The kids are decent, and it's nice to have interaction. I also enjoy reading history. I'm still involved with the intellectual stimulation of the job. Understanding literature and the ability to think critically is important.

Larry also finds having the summers off to be an attractive feature of teaching. "I like the idea of the free time that teaching should theoretically entail," he explains. Other reasons to remain in teaching stem from the support he has received this year from the department chair and the help from his colleagues. Although he observes that many of the faculty are "burned out" or just "putting in their time," he believes that the faculty in general is competent and friendly and that the interaction among the faculty is relatively good. He is also appreciative of the relatively stable neighborhood and school environment:

This is a good neighborhood. There's some discipline at the school, so I don't fear for my life. The students are poor academically, but it's not a rough neighborhood.

Good-Fit Leaver

David Jensen: "I never wanted to be completely out of the classroom." A former science teacher at Brown, David was first drawn to teaching by a positive volunteer experience:

I suppose I always liked transmitting information. A chemistry teacher encouraged me to do work in biology. I volunteered at a lab and ended up teaching volunteers. I learned I was good at it.

During his first year in teaching, David got married. Like other beginning teachers, he recalls receiving little formal assistance and struggling to make things work in the classroom, even postponing his honeymoon so he could mark exams. What did help him through the year were the informal discussions with his colleagues:

> I remember working very hard. I taught mainly the general core students. It was hard work. They were always given to the beginning teachers. I don't recall getting much help. I don't like being watched, and it was always awkward to observe. I remember getting advice around the lunch table. The high school was pretty lucky in science. We were a pretty close-knit group.

But by his fifth year, he had reached a point where he "could teach comfortably" and was confident of his effectiveness. His standard of success, however, was influenced by the advice of his former education professor: "Teachers can only reach a few kids in each class. If you reach one kid, consider yourself having done a good job."

Now, after 18 years in teaching, David has left the classroom and opened a camera business. His disenchantment with teaching was gradual. His colleagues and supervisor remember him as a very good and dedicated teacher who spent long hours on his work. He generally taught the motivated, above-average students. After about his tenth year of teaching, he became a counselor and taught only two classes a day. He did this for 8 years and received more satisfaction from working with students in a counseling capacity than as a teacher: "I really felt I was helping kids in one-to-one counseling to get medical attention. I felt I was helping more than in the classroom."

During his 15th year, David "started having second thoughts about teaching." He became disillusioned with the possibilities for advancement when a district-level promotion opportunity he believed he deserved opened up, but he did not get it:

> My principal, for whatever reasons, created a stumbling block to my getting out [of the school]. I was always brought up with the belief that hard work would lead to advancement. That doesn't happen. I worked hard and wanted the district administration position. It would've been right down my alley. But the powers that be didn't think so. I'd been a conscientious teacher and had a file eight inches thick of wonderful letters. But it wasn't worth a hill of beans. I really felt fired when I didn't get the district job.

As a white male, David also expressed frustration with the affirmative action policies that favored women and minorities "who couldn't read or write or speak English" over him:

> I was very happy in teaching. Then the racial business started, and that led to my disillusionment. I was very naive. I thought someday I would be a department chair or assistant principal. Then I realized around year 10 or 11 that it wouldn't happen. I started to look around, and white Jewish boys were the low men on the totem pole.

His desire for promotion stemmed not only from the need for recognition, but also from the need to do something different. He was not looking to leave teaching entirely, but he wanted an opportunity to do new things:

> I was looking for prestige and the idea of doing something a little out of the ordinary [for a teacher]. Teachers do get burned out. There have to be other places for teachers to fit and do something useful. I'd reached the point where I could do my job blindfolded and could do any lesson cold. That's not good for any teacher or student.
>
> I didn't see my future totally out of the classroom — maybe three or five years or less. What was important was the opportunity to do other things. I liked the idea of teaching others to teach. I liked the idea of some administration. I never wanted to be completely out of the classroom. I was not totally disillusioned with teaching.

David's disappointment with his lack of advancement was only one of several factors that led to his decision to leave. His last couple of years in the classroom were very unhappy. He was assigned to teach an advanced course in biology, which was not his field:

> I knew nothing about it [advanced biology], and I fought to get out of it. It wasn't a service to the kids. I could maybe have taught general biology, but not the advanced course. I was worried because it wasn't fair to the kids, but nobody cared. None of the parents complained. In an affluent system, parents would get upset at this, but not at our school.

David also felt frustration and resentment over the selection of the new department chair, a man who knew nothing about chemistry:

> In our department, the chair, who was the greatest human being, retired. The person who took his place was less knowledgeable and had less experience. He did biology, not chemistry. This created friction for those of us who had been there.

We didn't feel he was competent to tell us how to teach. That was very demoralizing.

It was this new department chair who assigned David to teach out of his field — an action that prompted David to take a sabbatical to explore other job possibilities. He had always worked part time outside the school, but he found he could not expand his part-time jobs into a full-time one. Then a friend who had been looking into opening a business suggested the camera shop. He decided to trade the security of teaching for the risk of a new business:

> If I'd the opportunity to move into the district-level job, it would've convinced me to stay, but I didn't and I needed to try something while I was still young enough.

David was also feeling pressure from his family to earn more money, and he believed that opening his own business carried such a potential. Two years after quitting teaching, David earns about as much as he did as a teacher. Yet he would return to the classroom only if his business failed. "I would not be looking forward to [returning to teaching]," he admits.

Weak-Fit Stayers

Sara Cohn: "To experiment with another job would be costly." Like many weak-fit teachers, Sara Cohn slipped into teaching almost by accident:

> I don't know why I became a teacher except when I went through the college catalogue, what I was most interested in were the history courses. It was as simple as somebody saying, "you don't need many credits to become a social studies teacher." I didn't consider other careers and wasn't really influenced by others in deciding.

Sara spends 40 hours a week on her work: teaching five periods of sophomore and junior history. A supervisor rates her work as "average." Sara took a 6-year leave of absence to stay home with the two children she now raises alone. She has been teaching for 19 years and says it is quite likely she will remain in the profession. Still, she is frustrated at not being able to do her job:

> I would like to go into the classroom and teach. I used to feel periods should be longer. But kids were different before. I can't

hold them for longer than 35 minutes. I'm just as happy to see them go at the end of the day.

Maybe in the boroughs there are some good schools where I could delve into ideas and be really teaching, trying to deal with values and getting into interesting stuff. Here at this school I do lessons on a much simpler level and don't go anywhere.

Class size and the kind of students prevent her from drawing satisfaction from her work:

In history we are doing the American Revolution. The kids say, "It's boring." They don't do the homework. In one class today, three did their homework.

I want fewer kids. Classes are capped at 34, but it's still too many for this school. Kids leave with books and we never see them again. I haven't seen one kid in months, and they think they can pass doing 20 days of work if they missed 40 days. They ask, "If I do work now, can I pass?" There should be a point of no return.

Sara also complains about the multiple roles teachers are asked to perform in her inner-city school and the insufficient support for this:

The guidance program is ineffective and idealistic. The amount that they do and their success rate are not high. The school is being asked to do more things than should be asked. Services we're asked to do are not teacher functions to do — they're more like social work.

Her frustrations with the workplace have affected her sense of professional competence. When asked about her effectiveness in the classroom, she replied:

I don't know about my effectiveness. I'm still working on manners. Kids are coming in late. They don't sit quietly; they move furniture, slam books on the desk, and say "hi" to friends.

Her depression about her job is reflected in how she contrasts Brown to another working-class high school she used to teach in: "At my old school, . . . it was stimulating and people were not hot to leave right after school. Here people start to leave early. They want to get out and forget it."

Although teaching at Brown is frustrating and dissatisfying, Sara is not looking for another school or another job. She lives within walking distance of the school, and the benefits of teaching fit nicely with her role as a single mother. When asked why she was staying in teaching, she replied:

> I have young kids and no financial independence. To experiment with another job would be costly. I'm not a free person. My interests revolve around my children. I have an adequate salary, health benefits, and security — unless I flip I won't be fired. That's my primary reason for staying.
>
> The second reason is that the hours are good for a mother although I have some tight arrangements to make in sending the kids off in the morning. The third is the work with students. This used to be at the top of my list.

Fred Baker: "If I reach one or two kids a year, I'm doing good."
Fred joined the Peace Corps in the 1960s and taught in a Southeast Asian high school for 2 years. When he returned to the United States, he decided to continue teaching to avoid the draft. His first job was as a regular substitute in a white, working-class school. After 3 years he was transferred to Brown. In his early years of teaching he came to the conclusion that if he "reached one or two kids a year," he would be "doing good." He also pursued other jobs, although he eventually concluded he was "not the type for business," since he was unwilling "to put on a gray-striped suit," nor was he willing to move from New York City. An affable man, Fred has never regretted staying in teaching because the low demands of teaching suit his personality well:

> I'm basically a lazy person. I'm not a hustler and not dedicated to my job. I'll do it and come in reasonably well prepared, [but] I tend to work slowly and must have my coffee every now and then.

Now a veteran of nearly two decades in teaching, Fred teaches remedial reading and study skills labs that require very little preparation; he works fewer than 40 hours a week. His supervisor rates him as "below average" as a teacher. Fred acknowledges that he gets "pretty lousy feedback from his supervisor — nothing positive."

Fred, who is single, intends to stay in teaching. His reasons have to do with his age and the lack of comparable alternatives: "I'm 40 and too old to be doing anything else. I don't think I'm really equipped for anything else within this pay. What else would I do?"

The job security, the salary (he earns about $40,000 a year), the summers off to travel, and the easy workload are powerful incentives to remain in the profession. He is so locked into teaching that he jokes that it would take "an earthquake" to push him out of it. Teaching is comfortable, requires little involvement, and suits Fred well.

The satisfaction he receives from the job derives from things external to the classroom. His salient rewards are the free evenings at home to listen to opera and the summers to go camping. The classroom work is something to put up with. He characterizes his students as the "dregs," "at the bottom of the barrel" in terms of ability. Fred complains that students are constantly late or absent, despite his threats to fail them. He believes that the students themselves prevent him from being more effective.

Another major impediment to his effectiveness is the lack of administrative support, having "the feeling that the administration is on your side, that they are there to help the student and teacher." Even though Fred likes teaching because of its low demands on him, at the same time he expresses regret at the lack of constructive criticism and encouragement to improve his performance. Fred describes his frustration with the administration's lack of support and its laissez-faire attitude toward teachers as long as classes are quiet:

> Nobody really cares what goes on in the classroom. If the class is quiet, if I don't murder, maim, or rape students, nobody cares. I would like them to worry about what I'm doing in positive ways. I'd like to see administrators be more involved in my teaching as opposed to observing me once or twice for bad points.

Susan Dodd: "I need more of a challenge where I can learn."
When Susan Dodd graduated from college with an English major, she could not think of anything to do with her degree except teach. Her father had told her many times that there was "nothing better in the world to do than be a teacher." Her first job was in what she called "a bombed-out black ghetto" in New York. She had no education courses or student teaching behind her when she started out. The stress of that first year was so intense that she lost 12 pounds and broke her wedding engagement. She received little help from her colleagues and made many mistakes. But her relationship with the students kept her going:

> The students were all-caring and protecting me. [But] I had no other support. When I asked teachers to see their lesson plans, they didn't share their work. The assistant principal was crazy and screamed at me. The only joy I had was the kids. I didn't

know what I was doing — I tried to teach pronouns and then
realized I hadn't taught nouns first.

Her sense of failure made her even more determined to continue in
teaching, but only for one more year — to prove that she could do it and
to heal her wounded self-esteem.

I changed schools the second year. I knew I couldn't overcome
a bad reputation at the first school. I kept going because I
didn't want the feeling of doing something badly. I was going
to teach a second year and then never walk into a school again.

However, her experiences the second year convinced her to return.
The principal was understanding and trusting, and she gained self-
confidence in her abilities. She remembers: "I was so good after the
second year; I was organized — that was of primary importance, and the
kids still liked me."

An "outstanding teacher" according to a school administrator, Susan has been teaching for 17 years now and plans to stay with it. Presently, she teaches only two courses a day and spends the rest of her time
doing course advising. This arrangement will end in 5 years when the
advisory position will be awarded to another teacher. Although she does
not want to leave teaching altogether, neither does she want to return to
teaching five periods a day. Thinking about her future, she says she
might want to be a dean of students, but that being an administrator is
unappealing because she is reluctant to relate with her colleagues as a
superior.

When her teaching career was interrupted by the births of her two
children, Susan took a 5-year leave of absence. Originally she had intended to stay out longer, until her youngest was in school, but decided
that she preferred to be in the classroom with students rather than at
home with toddlers. During her third year back in the classroom, she
recalls, she came "to truly love teaching." It was an exciting time for her;
for the first time she found herself in a supportive school environment.

The principal was fabulous — a mentor and a friend combined.
Everyone worked together. During free periods we did our
plans together. I still do plans with one of those teachers, Gretchen. We share: Two heads are better than one!

Her close professional and social relationship with Gretchen, also a
highly respected English teacher, has lasted 14 years. Best friends, Gretchen and Susan rely on each other for personal and professional support. They transferred to Brown together. They ride the same subway to

school in the morning, have lunch together every day, and spend vacations together to plan curriculum. Susan and Gretchen also became
grade counselors at the same time. Even though being a grade counselor
initially meant more work, Susan volunteered for the position because
she needed a change and wanted more personal contact with the students, most of whom do not have easy lives:

> I needed something new and different. I'd been teaching a
> long time. I wanted to deal with students on a different level,
> where I'm not threatening to them. For example, a student
> who didn't get along with me as a teacher because he didn't do
> his work is now a friend.

Susan likes her school and her colleagues. She appreciates the safety
and organization at Brown and thinks highly of her colleagues:

> I've been in lots of schools. This school's a very safe place. There
> are no intruders, and that's rare in New York City. A large
> number [of the faculty] have been here since the beginning and
> don't know what it's like to be in a school with no structure—
> [with] smoking in the halls and banging on the doors.
>
> This school has excellent teachers with good standards.
> Every day we're working together for a better school. Brown's
> less likely to tolerate teachers who aren't good. Sometimes the
> administration's a little too one-sided, not flexible. But it's
> better than the other way. [And] the English Department fac-
> ulty is always there for one another.
>
> Colleagues are the largest source [of my professional de-
> velopment]. We have a very professional [English] department.
> They enjoy what they do and share it.

With only two classes to prepare for, Susan spends about 42 hours a
week on her work these days. Her involvement in her job is constrained
by her other roles in life—that of wife and mother. Her husband resents
the time she spends on her work at home, and one of her children has
special needs that demand much of Susan's attention. Feeling guilty and
torn between her loyalties to family and students, she confesses, "I feel
I'm not good at both [teaching and homemaking]."

Although Susan considers herself a career teacher and wants to
continue teaching, the competing demands of the job and of family life
make her reluctant to return to a regular five-period teaching schedule
when her counseling position expires.

Weak-Fit Leavers

Gerald Craig: "I never had a sense of accomplishment." A former math teacher, Gerald Craig never had a strong desire to be a teacher. After college he could have pursued graduate work in mathematics, but chose not to. According to him, he entered the profession by happenstance: "There was a need for teachers in the early 1960s. There was a job, and I was there and did it. If there was a warm body, you got the job."

His first year of teaching, at a school located on one of the worst blocks in New York, was "a lot of sweat and aggravation." The first week he came home and broke down crying. He knew nothing about teaching and no one offered any help. He was left to his own devices:

> I learned how to handle it. I figured it out. Nobody helped me. There was no team teaching. It was sink or swim. There was phenomenal turnover — seven transfers in one year for a single position.
>
> The first month on the job I was on duty in the courtyard. I took a cigarette from a kid and got stabbed. The principal's letter to me was, "I hope you've learned your lesson." It was jungle warfare.
>
> I learned the tricks. In those days, you could hit a kid to establish authority. That's how I earned respect.

He never started out to be a teacher and "never took the system seriously," so when he took the licensing test to teach in high school, he never even studied for the exam.

Gerald taught for 18 years before quitting 3 years ago. For 12 of those years in the classroom, he also had a business repairing cars on the side. The administrator at Brown remembers Gerald as below average, someone "whose heart was not in teaching." He was at school from 8:30 A.M. to 2:50 P.M. every day. He said, "I worked 6 hours and 20 minutes [each day]. I was paid for that time and I didn't work any more [than that]."

During his 14 years at Brown, he did try to be creative and innovative. He developed a job-training program and became its administrator. This gave him a schedule with only two periods of teaching. The position, however, did not sustain his need for challenge and change, so he repaired cars on the side:

There were no challenges. The job was routine. I straddled the fence between being in business for myself and working for somebody else [in the public schools].

Finally, Gerald claims, he "fell from favor" with the principal, and the program was given to someone else. He was assigned a full teaching load once more. In his job as manager of the job-training program, he had fewer classroom duties. Other teachers suspected that he left campus during the school day to conduct his private business. When he returned to the regular classroom schedule, his "freedom of movement was cut." Only 6 months later, he took a leave of absence to conduct his business full time.

He had originally intended to return to Brown, but with some distance from his school experience he came to realize that he would not return to teaching. His primary reason centered on the lack of a sense of self-worth and accomplishment.

After 18 years of working hard at the craft, I never had a sense of accomplishment. I can [only] count a couple of good kids [that I had]. My work did not give me a sense of accomplishment.

Another major reason for not returning to teaching was the lack of recognition:

There are no rewards for a good job, and I don't necessarily mean money. Our energy and efforts are taken for granted and not appreciated. The system treats you as an infant.

Since he is his own boss and has a sense of accomplishment from his work, Gerald likes what he is doing now. He also makes much more money. While higher earnings were a factor in his decision to quit, he emphasized that was not the major reason. Gerald also was emphatic that he "would not return to teaching under any conditions." He believes he made the right decision to leave and that other teachers wish they could do the same. When visiting his best friend, who still works at Brown, Gerald observes: "The teachers there make no attempt to hide their envy. They say how lucky I am. It's sad. Their feelings aren't masked."

Marilyn Moore: "I feel battered."   Marilyn graduated from college in the 1950s, a time when "teaching and nursing were the only things I could think of for women to do." Her mother was a teacher, and she became one, too.

Marilyn began work at a music and art school where she put in long hours teaching, producing plays, and advising the yearbook staff. She recalls those years as "totally absorbing" and "terribly draining." After seven years she left the profession to become an actress but found "the [acting] field was sewn up." Ten years later she returned to teaching, having learned that she had "unrealistic expectations" about an acting career. She regrets none of her theater years and is glad she had no family to support, a situation that gave her the freedom to leave teaching.

Now in her late forties, Marilyn has taught for 17 years. Although a competent English teacher, she is preparing to leave public school teaching by getting a master's degree, which will enable her to teach in a community college. She is also actively seeking and applying for other jobs. Marilyn reports she has received positive feedback at Brown from her department chair and other teachers who have observed her. She believes she is effective, but only, she adds, "within the constraints." Two of the constraints are the inadequate time for preparation and the lack of appropriate materials for the special needs of her students.

Other major constraints have to do with workload: accommodating large classes with intensely needy students and constant discipline problems, working with students that even the police are unable to handle. If class sizes were smaller—somewhere under 25—and if Marilyn felt that she were reaching students instead of managing large groups, she would reconsider leaving:

> I go into class. I'm needed by all. They all need you. All have a note for you and a story to tell you. There are too many kids. Six or seven want to go to the bathroom or have an emergency. I sign notes and that could take 20 minutes and ruin the beginning of the class by creating confusion.
>
> It's a constant adjustment, every period, [with] new problems and new needs. It's exhausting—that hello and goodbye stuff—when periods are only 40 minutes.
>
> I spend all of my time on discipline. It's all about behavior, even in the honors classes. Kids are extremely emotionally needy, jealous of each other, hungry emotionally, aggressive, fearful adolescents. Their behavior's becoming wilder and wilder with each passing year.

In the ninth or tenth year after her return to teaching, Marilyn found herself exhausted and under tremendous stress:

I got to the point where I couldn't stand it if somebody wanted
to stay after and ask me questions or was in extreme need. I
had no patience if a sub[stitute] needed some help and felt like
screaming. I felt like I was on a tight rope. I needed to conserve
every gram of my energy.

These days Marilyn spends about 48 hours a week on her work. She says
she spends most of her time at home mainly recovering, "unwinding and
cooling out." She explained: "Here [at school] it's a war. We want to cut
it off when we get home. I feel battered."

With the exception of teachers who do not have a full five-period
load, she believes other teachers at Brown share her experience and
feelings. Other teachers, however, are not as emotionally spent as she is
because, according to Marilyn, they are "fatalistic" about their work
conditions. She contrasts her professional concerns to the family concerns of other teachers: "Their primary agenda is their family. Teaching
isn't really a career for them. They aren't concerned . . . professionally."

The lack of recognition is another major reason that Marilyn gives
for leaving teaching:

You're an invisible person. Outside of our department chair
this year, nothing is given in terms of recognition. [Instead]
there's constant blame, [for example] if I didn't lock the door or
shut the window at the end of the day.

Related to this problem of recognition is the low social status that teachers are accorded by society in general and her friends in particular:

At social functions, people discount you when you say you're a
teacher. Your friends who make more money and get more
recognition look down on you and wonder why you're still
teaching.

Yet Marilyn believes that her work is an important social service, even
though she lacks a sense of accomplishment or success. "I feel you're
fighting the good fight [as a teacher]," she says. "I don't feel I win, but
I'm not wasting my time here."

Still another major factor pushing Marilyn out of teaching is the
professional and social isolation she experiences in teaching. She explained:

[Teaching] is too isolating. I want camaraderie and contact
with people. I'm looking into college teaching . . . where I
could have some connection with people. I miss having a com-

munity where people visit you if you're absent and ask about you when you're gone. If any teacher left, we would forget all about that person here. [Even] when teachers clock out at the end of the day, nobody misses them. There's no community of professionals here. I need a community and want to be part of a family.

Another major concern is the scarcity of opportunities for professional improvement, what Marilyn calls the "dead-end quality" of teaching. She notes that teachers consequently turn outside of teaching for their stimulation and reward: "After 17 years, there's nothing to look forward to except more of the same. We must cultivate outside interests to endure the staleness and stress of the job." For Marilyn that means pursuing her own writing.

Although she speaks bitterly about teaching, Marilyn assesses her satisfaction as a 4 on a 7-point scale: "It sounds like I'm bitterly unhappy, but sometimes I am pleased. I [do] have grateful students who love me and I have a lot of positive experiences."

"The salary's adequate," Marilyn says, "but the rewards with kids are less and less." In the end, she still feels "uncompensated for the extraordinarily difficult work." The declining rewards from students, the lack of recognition and stimulation, and the lack of collegial interaction have resulted in Marilyn's resolve to leave public school teaching.

SUMMARY

The spotless, orderly halls at Brown give visitors the impression that the school runs as smoothly and efficiently as a well-oiled machine. But from interviews with present and former members of the faculty, a more complex picture emerges. The same management style that provides the much-valued buffer from external discipline problems also is perceived as stultifying professional discretion and growth and creating distrust between the faculty and administration. Bureaucratic, top-down control elicits faculty complaints about lack of stimulation and meaningful input in decisions that negatively impact professional involvement.

Brown faculty speak frequently of the difficulty of their work with inner-city students who bring diverse and intense educational and personal needs with them into the classroom. Many teachers feel overwhelmed by the challenge of working with these students in the context of large class sizes; few are rewarded by a sense of success for their efforts.

Brown provides a safety valve for some of the faculty in the form of nonteaching roles that effectively reduce the individual's workload. Rather than being a real solution, however, these measures provide only temporary relief and serve to mask the underlying disenchantment that even some of the good-fit faculty have with a normal teaching load at the school. Those who can manage it seek some form of escape, by leaving either the profession or the classroom (for nonteaching roles). Others simply withdraw emotionally, thus creating a perception of widespread dissatisfaction.

CHAPTER 3

Teaching in a Wealthy Suburb: Rolling Hills High School

"If you can't teach here, you can't teach," asserts veteran math teacher Dan Joffrey, reflecting a common view among the faculty that Rolling Hills is an excellent place to teach. Situated in a wealthy suburb in the San Francisco Bay Area, Rolling Hills belongs to a small high school district currently serving 9,000 students; only 6 years ago nearly 14,000 were enrolled. The decline is due to falling birth rates, combined with the fact that homes are too expensive for most young families with children. Starting prices for modest homes in the area in 1986 were $180,000; what a teacher referred to as "hovels" sold for $130,000. The houses in the immediate vicinity of the school fell within the $200,000 to $300,000 range. Couples with children and sufficient financial resources deliberately choose to live in this district due to the fine reputation of its schools.

Rolling Hills is noted for being "the most academic" among the district's five high schools. The school is located in a quiet residential section of town, where homes are hidden behind walls and hedges. A mile away, four lanes of fast traffic stream past high-rise office buildings and specialty shops selling computers and croissants. Built in the early 1970s, the school's buildings are fashioned from attractive red brick and roofed in typical California Spanish tiles. Rolling Hills, having the luxury of space in the suburbs, intersperses small courtyards and trees among its low-lying buildings, creating pleasant spots for students to congregate between classes. A football field, swimming pools, and tennis and basketball courts are situated at the south end, which opens onto an expansive grassland offering a panorama of gentle foothills.

The declining number of students and Proposition 13, a state tax-reduction initiative that slashed funds available for education, forced the school district to lay off teachers in 1980 and again in 1984, resulting in the "graying" of the work force. In the entire district, only a dozen teachers have 5 or fewer years of teaching experience. In the near future, this configuration will change radically. By 1991, Rolling Hills

High School will need to hire replacements for the nearly one third of its 87 teachers who are planning to retire.

Relations between the site administration and faculty are cordial. Previously a district-level administrator, Barbara Lee has been principal at the school for only 2 years and has already earned a reputation for being open and fair. In this era of fiscal retrenchment, the union is very influential and actively participates in shaping district policies. For example, the union proposed and successfully negotiated a seven-period day in order to maintain elective courses in the curriculum.

A high pay schedule and substantial benefit package characterize this school district. A teacher who has a master's degree and has taught for 28 years earned $43,000 in 1986. In addition, the district offers full family, dental, medical, vision, and prescription coverage. By contrast, a teacher at Brown with the same qualifications made approximately $3,500 less; at Roosevelt, a similar teacher earned about $5,000 less.

COMMUNITY CHARACTERISTICS:
STUDENT COMPOSITION AND ACHIEVEMENT

The student body at Rolling Hills is comprised of 1,950 students, of whom 80% are white, 15% Asian, 4% Hispanic, and 1% black. Most of their parents have professional, often management-level, jobs in nearby high-tech computer industries.

The library's special room that houses the substantial collection of brochures and catalogues from colleges and universities across the nation signals a strong emphasis on college attendance. In fact, 50% of the students enroll in 4-year institutions of higher learning; half of these students attend prestigious 4-year colleges, such as Ivy League schools and those in the University of California system. Forty percent of the graduating class go on to 2-year colleges, many preferring to attend the excellent community college in the vicinity and later transferring to a 2-year institution. Some students enter the job force directly; very few join the military or enroll in vocational training.

The capabilities of the students and the academic emphasis at Rolling Hills are evident in its high standing statewide and nationally. The graduating class of 1985 produced seven National Merit semifinalists; the California Achievement Program, a test that permits comparison of student achievement across schools, placed Rolling Hills students in the 93rd to 96th percentile. Unlike the situation at most other secondary schools, student attrition from ninth grade until graduation is negligible at Rolling Hills.

The student body is so homogeneous academically that nearly three-fourths (73%) of the teachers responded that they had no classes containing significant numbers of students with limited English or students who are 3 years below grade level in reading or math. So few of the recent Asian immigrants at the school have special language needs that Rolling Hills offers only one English-as-a-second-language (ESL) class, which serves only 15 students. This may somewhat underestimate the true need, however, as parents, mindful of college entrance requirements, push to have their children quickly integrated into regular classes and prefer not to have ESL courses registered on the transcripts. About 200 other students require special education assistance, and most of these are also mainstreamed into regular classes.

Parents actively participate in the life of the school, and more than three-quarters of the faculty (78%) indicated satisfaction with the level of parental support. Nearly all of the families are represented at the freshmen orientation in September. More than half of the upper-grade parents attend the annual open house. They lend their presence, energies, and financial resources to such activities as the music booster club (supporting both the choral and instrumental groups and their performances abroad), the athletic booster clubs for each sport, and the college nights and graduation parties.

Parents also volunteer to come to school each day after lunch to help telephone the parents of absentee students—a task usually requiring less than an hour due to the infrequency of absences. The official figures peg student attendance at 97% to 98%; however, a teacher pointed out that these numbers somewhat overestimate actual attendance, as students are allowed to make up certain absences, including those due to family vacations. Still, a math teacher estimated that he generally has as few as one or two absences a week in his upper-level courses. Table 3.1 summarizes major characteristics of Rolling Hills High School.

WORKLOAD AND SOURCES OF STRESS

Although class sizes at Rolling Hills, with about 33 students per teacher, are nearly identical to those at Brown, complaints from Rolling Hills faculty about student-teacher ratios are muted or indirect. Part of this is due to a conscious strategy by the union to win higher pay in exchange for maintaining present class loads. Much of the explanation also lies in the fact that Rolling Hills' homogeneous suburban student body dramatically differs from the high-need, heterogeneous student body in the inner city. This is not to argue that the faculty at Rolling

TABLE 3.1. Summary of School Characteristics, Rolling Hills High School

Location: San Francisco suburb
Grades: 9-12
Number of teachers employed full time: 87
Average class size: 33
Number of students enrolled in September 1986: 1,950
Ethnicity of students: 20% Asian, Hispanic, & black; 80% white
Ethnicity of faculty: 96% white
Student socioeconomic status: High-income professional parents
Daily student absences: 2-3%
Dropout rates: Negligible

Hills have an easy job, only that the task of teaching is very different here.

Teaching at Rolling Hills is not without its own sources of stress. Pressure from the administration to cover a certain amount of curriculum within a given time period produces intense strain. Mary Baker, a mentor teacher in the science department who plans on staying in teaching because nothing else gives her "the psychological and emotional lift that teaching does," related how teaching at Rolling Hills can take a toll on the individual:

> I really feel the bell to bell pressure. . . . We have so much to cover. The administration is picky about starting at the bell and ending at the bell. If there's a phone call or a question from the student [at the break], I sometimes miss the bathroom call.
>
> School is from 7:50 A.M. to 3:10 P.M. In the summer, I work [as a lab technician] from 7:20 to 4:30, but I am not one-tenth as tired as I am from teaching. There is mental stress at not being able to work at one's [own] rate.

Evelyn Brown, a well-regarded English teacher with 16 years of experience who enjoys the creative aspect of teaching, agreed that the time and workload demands produce high stress: "I feel my job is extremely stressful. I stay up till 10:00 or 11:00 [at night] and am up at 4:00 in the morning [to correct papers]." Indeed, more than half of the faculty (56%) identified the task of correcting papers as a major source of stress at Rolling Hills.

A source of frustration unexpected in this affluent setting is the shortage of materials. A social studies teacher complained about having to photocopy materials because the school cannot afford to buy new books. A new science teacher, who transferred from a private school, offered that although many enabling conditions were in place in the school, the shortage of learning materials (for example, "decent, working microscopes" essential to her biology labs) is the major impediment to her effectiveness in the classroom. Less than half of the Rolling Hills faculty (46%) indicated that they were satisfied with the adequacy of materials for classroom use, a percentage nearly identical to that reported by Brown faculty (44%).

The other side of having high levels of parental support is, as social studies teacher Patrick Valley put it, that "the school [administration] is unbelievably concerned about parent responses." Too many parent complaints will trigger close scrutiny by the administration. "Parents and students want a lot and they get a lot," added Dan Joffrey, but parents are sometimes "too pushy," producing "stress and pressure" on the teacher. Dan estimated that he receives a call a week from parents complaining about their children's grades.

Carl Fisher, a business and science teacher who is planning on retiring from teaching earlier than he had originally intended because of "the general stress of teaching," is intensely dissatisfied with the low level of parental support that he receives when students have problems:

> There are continuous annoyances, little problems that never get solved. [For example,] I contact a parent about a student not achieving, and the parent isn't concerned or says that it's my fault.

Although parents generally are involved in school activities, Dan Joffrey, a highly rated math teacher, expressed his frustration with the relative inattention of parents to teaching values and the growing expectation that teachers assume parenting roles:

> Things are thrown on teachers because parents want to make their $100,000 instead. For example, we have to teach values. I have a good relationship with parents, but no one's home after school and kids are left to do what they want. I'm frustrated about the increasing expectations for teachers when at the same time the public will vote no funding for education.

Student noninterest in social and political issues is a source of major frustration and stress for Bruce Jenson, a veteran social studies teacher who admits to having great "ego involvement" in his subject matter.

Bruce has no discipline problems with the students and considers them nice kids, "spoiled, but decent." Yet he is extremely frustrated in his attempts to get them to look at what he considers important issues:

> I can't get most of the students to look at Nicaragua. . . . Important issues are so difficult to do. They end up by saying that social studies is boring. I told a class we were involved in 1962 in a place called Vietnam. The kids' response was "who cares?"

Despite the workload and the perceived sources of stress, Rolling Hills faculty experience a high degree of efficacy in the classroom. Olga Lawrence captured a prevalent attitude among the faculty when she said: "I'm competent. I put in a lot of time and effort into [my teaching]. I feel very confident in it." Ninety percent of the faculty believed that they were able to accomplish their instructional goals with more than 60% of their students. Only 33% of the Brown faculty indicated the same. Moreover, 56% of Rolling Hills teachers reported feeling "very successful" in getting their students to learn, while only 26% of the teachers at Brown responded similarly.

PROFESSIONAL CONCERNS: RELATIONS WITH THE ADMINISTRATION

A common sense of goal unifies the school. Patrick Valley, who expects to stay in teaching, said that the fact that "the administration, teachers, and parents are concerned with academics" makes it easy for teachers to do their best in the classroom.

The faculty at Rolling Hills reveals little of the conflict between administration and faculty present at Brown. Mary Baker reflects a commonly held, benign view of faculty relations with the school administration:

> We have the best administrative staff. Nobody bugs you here with petty b.s. The school runs smoothly. The administration here gives you support for the kids who give you trouble.

Asked to evaluate Rolling Hills as a workplace, Betty Davidson, a special education teacher, focused on the accommodating and responsive attitude of the administration. In contrast to administrators in the district's other schools, Rolling Hills' managers truly "serve the teacher."

Olga Lawrence, who enjoys teaching so much that she feels her day "really flies," pointed out how administrative policies and practices support teachers' classroom effectiveness by protecting their time and putting real support behind the need for discipline.

> [The administration] is very good here about cutting down on useless meetings, [and] they have few rallies [which detract from class time]. They have good discipline policies on tardies. If a student is tardy three times they get written up and go to Saturday school. Also [they have good policies] for cheating. If someone's caught they get an "F" for the semester. These policies need to have meat behind them; students need to know that there are consequences.
>
> [In addition] there's a duplicating service here. If you give them something, they'll deliver it to your room in 2 days. That makes a teacher more effective. I don't need to do tedious or tiresome things.

Through their union, teachers at Rolling Hills play an active role in shaping policy regarding their working conditions. Nearly a third of the faculty (30%) indicated that they had been a union negotiator or representative at one time in their teaching careers, a high percentage compared to the two other schools. For example, the cut in janitorial services, the elimination of counselors, and the present class sizes were the result of negotiations by teachers who identified these as areas that could be sacrificed in exchange for higher salaries. Complaints, then, about these particular working conditions influencing a teacher's workload were generally muted, if mentioned at all. The high level of teachers' participation in the union and consequently in decision making seemed to be related to the high level of their satisfaction with the school.

In addition to the school's administrators, Rolling Hills' department chairs play a critical role in creating enabling conditions for teachers, acting as critical buffers for their teachers. When asked what school factors help her be effective in the classroom, an English teacher replied:

> Good department chairs. Our lives don't get encumbered by outside class demands. [The English department chair] heads off things and is the spokesperson on difficulties with expectations of teachers. He plays a political role as well as [assumes] academic leadership.

The Rolling Hills department chairs are regarded more as teacher-leaders than as an arm of the administration, as they are at Brown due to structural differences in the roles. At Rolling Hills, the department chairs receive either an extra stipend or a free period to perform their administrative duties; they are still part of the teachers' union and do not participate in the evaluation of teachers. Although department chairs are chosen by the administration, these positions rotate among enough of the teachers so that half of them have been chairs. On the other hand, Brown's department chairs are required to take a special test for the job, are paid on an administrative salary scale, evaluate teachers, and do not belong to the teachers' bargaining unit; only 10% of the Brown faculty have held such positions, many of them in a temporary capacity, filling in until someone meeting the special requirements is hired.

DISTRICT- AND STATE-LEVEL INFLUENCES

The series of layoffs among teachers and school policies resulting from shrinking fiscal resources dramatically altered the work experiences of certain teachers, especially those with relatively low tenure or in the nonacademic areas, such as home economics and industrial arts. Many were laid off not just once, but several times. Programs, especially in the elective areas, were slashed or eliminated altogether.

Valerie Green, an outstanding teacher who was once chair of the foreign language department and who left teaching in 1980, described the effects of declining resources on her work experience. As department chair, she increased the enrollment in language courses such that at one point the department had 1,000 students. Then the first wave of layoffs came, and all but two teachers were let go. Noncontract teachers with little experience in or low commitment to foreign languages were hired to replace those laid off, and the quality of instruction in the department plummeted. As department chair, Valerie was charged with resolving this problem and mollifying angry parents. Eventually she resigned from teaching in frustration because she was given no support in making the improvements necessary for a quality program.

The reduction in financial resources had the additional effect of assigning teachers in nonmajor areas to teach out of their field. An administrator explained how this created a problem for weak teachers:

> Prior to Proposition 13 [the state initiative that reduced funds available to education], there was more fat in the system and not all the teachers taught in a critical area. Since the cutbacks, everybody has to teach in a critical area and there's no place to hide anybody, so poor teachers stand out more. Every-

body['s competence or incompetence] has been visible these past 4 to 5 years.

PROFESSIONAL GROWTH

Rolling Hills teachers value opportunities to stretch themselves in a professional sense. Marvin Price, a highly regarded mentor teacher, said: "I'm fearful of being robotic. . . . I enjoy learning. I value the learning [as a teacher], [because] it forces me to continue to grow."

Professional growth opportunities occur in a variety of forms at Rolling Hills. Money is sometimes available for teachers to attend conferences in their academic areas. In addition, 2 days a year are set aside as professional development days by the district. For some veteran teachers the in-services offered by the district are of limited value.

According to Marvin Price, the district in-services that bring in experts unfamiliar with how things are done at the school often miss the mark in terms of teachers' needs and interests. Instead, an approach more useful to his development is the opportunity to "take a topic in a subject field, like graphing or estimation in math, and have teachers help other teachers with their ideas." He supports the union's proposal for a shortened schedule once a month to allow more time for departments to work together. Being able to take on different roles, such as department chair or mentor teacher, has also stimulated and encouraged Marvin to improve.

The differences between Rolling Hills and Brown in terms of opportunities for professional development are striking. Two-thirds of the Rolling Hills faculty (67%) reported that their opportunities for professional growth are "adequate"; less than a third of the faculty at Brown (29%) indicated their satisfaction in this area.

COLLEGIAL INTERACTION AND RELATIONS

At noon most of the teachers and administrators congregate in the faculty lunchroom, which quickly fills with friendly chatter. Science teacher Mary Baker explained that the strong cohesion among Rolling Hills' teaching staff is unusual in the district.

Faculty relationships are unique here because of the layoffs; lots of teachers have come and gone, so there are no cliques. At [another high school in the district] there are separate tables at lunch and you're asked to move if you sit at the wrong table. The faculty's pretty supportive as a whole, and is excited about teaching.

Recently union members went from school to school to explain our proposal for a seven-period day. Our faculty was very different from the rest. Others were suspicious of the plans or argumentative. You'll see at our faculty meetings, people make jokes, and there isn't tension.

While most teachers would agree with Mary, a few would not. Frequently observed eating alone in a tiny room adjacent to the lunchroom is Carl Fisher, a business and science teacher having trouble with discipline in his classes and rated as below average in effectiveness by an administrator. From Carl's perspective, the faculty members are indeed "cliquish." Comments about Carl by colleagues reveal an impatience and frustration with colleagues who do not pull their own weight and with the administration's inability to rectify the situation.

Being part of a strong faculty, especially on the department level, is the source of much pride and an important reason to continue in the profession. Explaining why he will stay in teaching, Dan Joffrey related:

> I like this school. There are great kids and this is the best department in the district. There are excellent teachers and we have a good, solid math program. All the kids tell us they are super well prepared for college. I am part of a good team.

Teachers here speak frequently about the effects of collegial exchange and collaboration on their professional development. In the science department, for example, Olga Lawrence noted a "willingness to coteach and share ideas," which she finds extremely stimulating. Dan Joffrey reported that planning and teaching the same math course with a colleague keeps him on his toes and helps generate new ideas. Financial incentives, when available, are given for teachers to plan and develop curriculums together during the summer.

TEACHING CAREERS AT ROLLING HILLS HIGH SCHOOL

Despite the pressures of a highly academic environment, Rolling Hills High School is a pleasant place to teach. As social studies teacher Patrick Valley said, it has "a good working environment," the only problems being the declining enrollment and funding. Here the vast majority of the faculty (81%) are satisfied with teaching. Mary Baker verbalizes her colleagues views in this way: "I'm satisfied with the job and myself after work. I eagerly look forward to going to work in the morning." Victor Thomas, a 64-year-old veteran, put it more simply: "I like the kids and like what I do. Teaching's a worthwhile career."

Whereas the climate among teachers at Brown is one of dissatisfaction, at Rolling Hills it is quite positive: 74% of the Rolling Hills faculty, compared to only 32% of the Brown faculty, believe that their close colleagues are satisfied with teaching.

Rolling Hills has a very low voluntary turnover rate. Although nearly a third of the teachers plan to retire in the next 5 years, only 6% of the faculty are likely to quit for other reasons. Given the nearly ideal conditions at the school, what might explain why teachers leave? And how is it that some teachers are dissatisfied while the vast majority are not? A notable characteristic of the majority of leavers from Rolling Hills is that they teach in nonmajor subject areas, such as home economics, foreign languages, and industrial arts. (Table 3.2 lists the major characteristics of the 17 teachers interviewed.) What accounts for this phenomenon?

Good-Fit Stayers

Evelyn Brown: "We need a support system to use our abilities."
Evelyn Brown's father was a minister who taught his two daughters to enjoy intellectual discussion and to value schooling and service. Both Evelyn and her sister became teachers.

Although a teacher for 16 years, Evelyn is one of the younger faculty members at Rolling Hills. A dedicated literature and writing teacher, Evelyn spends nearly 60 hours a week on her school work. She considers her job extremely stressful because of the long hours that are required. Evelyn, who is single, spends her summers in school-related activities, either taking classes or working for the teachers' association. Her supervisor evaluated her work as very good — "an 8 or 9 out of 10."

She remembers feeling like a failure her first year as a teacher. Although she worked hard, she felt that she did nothing right. She wanted to quit, but enough people encouraged her to remain:

> I had the encouragement of the department chair, who told me that I really only needed more experience. My sister told me the same. [And] I recall excellent moral support from col-

TABLE 3.2. Interviewees' Characteristics Rolling Hills High School (*n* = 17)

Name	Age	Years in Teaching	Subject Taught	Hours Worked Weekly	Supervisor Evaluation
GOOD-FIT STAYERS					
Dan Joffrey	47	17	Math	57	8.5
Marvin Price	36	15	Math	43	10
Patrick Valley*	39	15	Social Studies	56	8.5
Olga Lawrence	31	8	Science	45	7
Evelyn Brown*	38	16	English	58	8.5
GOOD-FIT UNDECIDED					
Tina Crosley	34	7	English	54	7.5
GOOD-FIT LEAVERS					
Bruce Jenson	50	25	Social Studies	40	7.5
Fabian Terrell	45	20	P.E./Science	45	6
Marsha Junkett†	33	11	Home Economics	53	8
Alice Judson†	48	16	P.E./English	58	6
Valerie Green*†	37	16	Foreign Language	53	8
WEAK-FIT STAYERS					
Betty Davidson*	40	18	Special Ed.	45	8.5
Victor Thomas	64	30	Social Studies	40	7.5
Mary Baker	40	17	Science	49	8.5
WEAK-FIT LEAVERS					
Vicky Breuner*†	36	13	Home Ec./Soc. St.	48	8
Carl Fisher*†	50	23	Business/Science	41	2
Oscar Lemmer†	50	25	Industrial Arts	40	5

*The interview with this teacher is included as a vignette.

†This teacher has already left the profession.

Note: Teachers who say they will quit teaching before they reach 55 years of age and before qualifying for full retirement benefits are considered leavers; teachers who say they will stay in teaching for 5 years but are not sure after that are considered "undecideds."

leagues. In my teaching program I had a circle of support to share things with and my immediate supervisor gave good, sound help.

In retrospect, although she felt badly about that first year, she recalls strong collegial support, and that experience set the foundation for her professional growth. Today she sees herself as an competent teacher who continues to improve:

I'm tested daily but overall I'm improving. I'm prepared to give a lot of energy to the individual style of the student. I now have more knowledge of different personalities and how to work with them. I can spot earlier when students need my attention. I can still be fooled by students, but it's not so serious. My skills in teaching have also sharpened.

Evelyn reflects on the factors that have supported the development of her effectiveness in the classroom throughout the years. She relies on collegial and administrative support and stimulation for her own professional development:

I'm involved in workshops to develop curriculum, but I need support from the administration to do that. It's not as frequent as it should've been during the last 16 years, but there is more lately.

We're sometimes supported financially to go to conferences such as the one sponsored by the California Association of Teachers of English. There's also in-service training. But the most valuable time is with colleagues to go over materials. It's best done in the summer because it's hard to keep going during the year. When there're funds, we sometimes get paid to do that.

Evelyn believes that, in addition to administrative support at the district or school level, department-level leadership is critical to the support system necessary to develop and sustain professional competence. Her department chair, for example, will protect her from outside demands on her time and will advocate on her behalf for opportunities to acquire new skills.

Evelyn plans on staying in teaching because she enjoys the challenge to create and learn and likes working with the students. "I like the atmosphere and imminence of learning," she explains. "Every year gives me growth since the population of students changes."

Her colleagues at Rolling Hills, a major source of stimulation and growth for Evelyn, are another important reason for remaining in teaching. According to her, colleagues are also a source of professional pride and identification:

The kind of teachers here are the kind I like to work with. They're the heart and soul of the community and are doing a lot of good. They aren't expecting material reward. I can get advice from people who are problem solvers. I admire most of the staff and am proud to associate with them.

Evelyn did not always think she would make teaching a career. About 10 years ago, when she had been in the classroom for 5 years, she looked for a way out of teaching and started training to be a social worker, a career that would still allow her to work with people and "to be accountable in human terms." She suspected that a job in social work would entail more bureaucracy than teaching, but she rationalized that she could get used to it because she had become so dissatisfied with teaching.

The reason Evelyn prepared herself to leave teaching was that she had become worn out and discouraged by her classes. For 3 years in a row she had been assigned three remedial writing classes with 30 to 35 students in each class. She might actually have left if the department chair had not finally given her some other classes. She needed that change to prevent what she remembers as "burnout." Even now, she requires periodic change to renew herself in the classroom. Today, since class sizes for writing courses have been decreased from 35 to 27, and since she has more experience, Evelyn believes she could handle the same schedule that made her seek other job alternatives. But as a young teacher, the assignments with remedial students and the large class sizes were overwhelming and nearly drove her from the profession.

Patrick Valley: "I stuck it out because I hoped to get a regular class."   Now almost 40 years old, Patrick entered the profession because he was inspired by a former teacher, "a dedicated, responsible person concerned about people and about doing a good job." Patrick shared those values and saw teaching as a service and kind of calling, something he could personally be successful at because of his people skills. He explains:

> I'm successful because I have those qualities which lead one to being a good educator. I have empathy, understanding, and concern about what's going on today. I'm concerned about the whole person.

Patrick has been teaching for 15 years and intends to remain in the classroom until retirement. He is pleased with the social studies classes he now has at Rolling Hills but hated his first 2 years in the classroom. The only job available was in special education, but he accepted it on the promise that he would eventually receive a regular assignment in his major. He described the stress of those early years due to the lack of support:

Teaching special ed[ucation] was an emotional and physical drag with no return. I couldn't see any progress and was basically babysitting. I had no power to deal with the environmental problems. It was a new program and there was no guidance about what to do. I had little support from colleagues and the administration. And had no support from parents. It's like night and day to compare that time with the support I get at this school now.

The frustrating experiences had a profound effect on his sense of professional efficacy:

I wanted to teach, but wasn't teaching. It wasn't an educational situation or setting. I was in a holding pattern with the kids. I felt I was giving all this stuff because I wanted to be empathetic, but there was nothing noticeable in return. No progress was being made — academic or social.

After putting up with special education for 2 years, Patrick was finally assigned to teach in his own field, and "every year since then has been super."

A highly rated teacher (an administrator rates him an 8 or 9 out of 10 in effectiveness) who works an average of 56 hours a week, Patrick believes he is extremely effective with his students: "I have responsive kids, and I'm difficult with them. I require them to do things. I demand quality work and time. I'm understanding, but I'm not easy to take advantage of."

His sense of efficacy is due not only to his individual qualities but also to a supportive school environment in which the administration, teachers, parents, and students are focused on a common goal — academic achievement. His reasons for staying in teaching center on the personal rewards of working with his students. The challenge and stimulation from the interaction with students make him feel 10 years younger and help him to be more aware of the needs of his own three children. Another important reward is his positive relationship with his department chair, who recognizes and respects his work. Finally, the salary is another reason to stay in teaching. Patrick makes over $40,000 a year and believes it would be difficult to get a new job in that range. "The idea that teachers are leaving for higher-paying jobs is an illusion," he adds.

Patrick's career in teaching was threatened when he was twice laid off due to district cutbacks. The first time he was reinstated immediately. The second time he had to substitute in the district for a year before regaining permanent status. Although bitter about the district's layoff process, he decided to remain in teaching. Both personal and professional reasons came to play in that decision. His age and fondness for summer travel, as well as his enjoyment of teaching, enabled him to persist under the uncertain job conditions.

> I was 38 years old and didn't want to make a career change. I saw no reason to move. I felt because of the [advanced] age factor at the school, there'd be retirements in 3 years. So I stuck around. I also enjoyed teaching. I didn't feel so personally about being laid off. I like the time off and the job itself. I was willing to take the risk to be rehired and possibly to be laid off again because the good outweighed the bad.

Like other good-fit stayers, Patrick has no desire to be an administrator because "administrators lose touch with the students."

Good-Fit Leaver

Valerie Green: "It was a sad ending to a neat profession." Valerie came to teaching through her love of Spanish. She studied the language in high school and went abroad to study it during college. With her language skills, teaching seemed a "natural" career and a practical choice as well. So she pursued a high school credential.

She married soon after graduation, moved to California, and got her first teaching job. She had a difficult year with six course preparations in addition to advising the Spanish Club, the debate team, and the Speech Club, but she remembers getting strong support from the department chair. She saw him everyday, and he always had suggestions for her. By the end of the year, she felt fairly good about her accomplishments.

She intended to stay only 2 or 3 years and then have a family, but the years passed quickly. After 5 years she divorced her husband and had to support herself financially. That was an "impetus to stay" longer, but she also remembers feeling good about being in teaching and thinking that she had invested a considerable amount in staying: "I had committed a lot of time and energy to teaching, and I really did enjoy it for the first 10 years."

Valerie taught Spanish for 16 years before she left teaching. For 11 of those years she was at Rolling Hills High School, serving as the department chair for part of that time. A highly committed and involved teacher, she worked more than 50 hours a week on the average.

speech therapist because she felt unsuccessful, even though people told her she was doing well.

> Everybody told me, "You're doing fine. You're [just] new." But I was uncomfortable. I left that job because I was expected to be an expert in too many things: stuttering, voice, articulation, etc. My personality doesn't deal with that. I wanted to be good at something.

The next few years were better because her new job did not demand such a wide range of expertise from her. Still she tried to get out of her field as an itinerant speech therapist by getting a credential to teach drivers' education — an area in which she could feel confident in her abilities. She explains: "I always thought to do something more structured so I could feel more secure in my field." But there were only summer openings in drivers' education. For the next 6 years, she took classes to prepare herself for other jobs, thinking that she would eventually change occupations.

> All this time I was convinced that teaching was not for me. I really felt I shouldn't have been in teaching because I wasn't here out of choice. I never felt comfortable. So I went to school to take classes, for example, in the travel industry to be a ticket agent, in bartending, and to be a sign language interpreter.

Finally, in 1974, she was offered a classroom job teaching communication for the handicapped. During the 7 years at this job, she stopped training for alternative jobs because she finally felt self-confident in her new work. She reasoned: "I was more comfortable [in this new job] and could be expert in this field. I thought, 'I can do this.'" Gradually, she realized that she wanted to stay in teaching until retirement.

In 1982, she got a resource specialist position in special education, which gave her one period free to test students and to do the mountain of paperwork required by the state. In addition to feeling secure in her expertise, Betty also came to appreciate the benefits and security in teaching. By this time, having reached her mid-thirties, she also felt less able to compete with younger people for alternative jobs:

> I realized in 1981 when I went for my master's that I wanted to stay in teaching. If I was going to stay I needed to get more education, and I had done enough looking around. I didn't think I was going to change jobs because of the security here.

As much as I looked [at other jobs], nothing intrigued me. After 18 years as a teacher, I would lose salary: I couldn't get a higher paying job on the outside, a benefit package, the nice vacations, and job security if I changed jobs. [Also] I would have to compete against younger people for the new job.

Besides the salary, vacation, benefits, and job security, Betty is staying in teaching because she enjoys working with most of her students. She says of her personal relationship with students: "I have a lot of rapport with the students. They can talk to me. I try to understand their problems."

Support from her peers and the administration is a main factor holding her in teaching.

People I worked with were a main reason I stayed. The message I got from them was that I was doing a wonderful job. Most people I deal with socially are still in education. My best friend's still in teaching.

People-wise, Rolling Hills is wonderful. There's a great administration. They serve the teacher. Administrators at other schools get caught trying to serve both the district office and the teachers. I have never asked for anything that has not been addressed by the administration. I don't get everything I want, but when I have problems with kids, the administrators come and give ideas about what to do.

There's a good support system. [But] I feel sorry for new teachers. You do have to ask or do leg work to get what you want.

The professional development offerings in the district have been ample for Betty and provide another inducement to stay. She took part in six in the recent year and will be paid to attend still another in the summer.

Although Betty plans on staying in teaching, she continues to take evening math classes on the chance that she may want to change subjects in the future. She explains: "It's fun to take courses and I like to go to school. I might like to teach math someday." Her comments on why she contemplates a change in subject areas illustrate the importance she places on a sense of efficacy:

I'm very effective as far as being a caring person. . . . [But] I'm not sure I'm teaching them anything. It's so hard to know because of special education. I go over and over things and then they get nothing on the competency test. So I question my effectiveness. Many times I don't find the right avenue or modality to teach them. I would rate myself as average in academic teaching and above average in relating with students.

Weak-Fit Leavers

Vicky Breuner: "Teaching can be a stifling atmosphere." Vicky recalls becoming a teacher because of parental pressure. Her mother was a teacher and assured her "it was a good job." But it was the salary that was the strongest draw to teaching.

It was mainly economics. I was just married and needed to support my husband. The salary was half-way decent for women. I started at $8,600 [in 1969]. I'd interviewed with a manufacturer in sales and would've gotten half the teaching salary. I'd also done small acting parts and did some modeling [but couldn't make a living from them].

Her first year of teaching was at a school in a working-class neighborhood. She remembers that year fondly:

It was real new and fresh and very rewarding. I had a love relationship with teaching. I already had the basic skills with students, especially those from lower socioeconomic families. They were all good people—the parents, too. Students were motivated to learn, not like students at Rolling Hills. The kids [at my first school] were much more honest and open about how they felt. They didn't manipulate as much. I felt good about that year. There was a close-knit feeling among a lot of us at that school.

Vicky taught for 13 years before she quit in 1982. In about her seventh year of teaching home economics, the district laid off teachers due to budget cuts, and she was "shoved into" teaching social studies, her minor. Often three out of her five courses were in history, a situation she did not relish. Vicky, now divorced and a financial consultant, was evaluated as a good teacher in her major but as "having trouble" in her minor.

Her feelings on leaving teaching contrast sharply with the optimism of her first year:

I felt horrendous about teaching when I left. I left against
parental pressure to stay. I'd stopped feeling good about teaching about half way into my career, but I stayed because other
things were working and I had a consistent salary.

I loved the kids, but the pressure I was under was horrendous. I was getting a skin rash. I told one class, "I feel too
much stress," and I left mid-year. Things were not working for
me.

I left because of administrative hassles. I like a creative
atmosphere and I had no ability to do what I needed to, for
example, the timing about things and administrators not being
open to ideas I had. [And] I didn't want to teach history.

Vicky had problems with administrators for several years before she
actually quit:

Administrators need to be much more considerate of creativity
in teaching and listen to teachers on a gut level, not a superficial level. I tried to block a lot of this administrative stuff out —
their reacting to teachers as numbers instead of people.

The process of leaving was gradual. Vicky first seriously considered
leaving during her seventh year, when she began teaching in her minor.
She started to sell real estate on the side. Teaching provided her with her
base salary, and business became her creative outlet on the weekends
and vacations. It was a satisfactory situation for a while, but by the
tenth year, she knew she would eventually have to leave teaching. She
transferred to Rolling Hills the next year, hoping that her situation
would improve. Two years later she quit in mid-year.

Having to teach social studies, an area in which Vicky felt much
less effective than in her major, was a critical factor in pushing her out
of the public schools. When she quit, she had several ideas for her next
career and had sufficient financial security to tide her over. She traveled
abroad for several months, made some important business contacts, and
returned home to start financial consulting.

She contrasts teaching to being in business by noting that teaching
lacked the freedom and stimulation that her work has now:

The jobs are similar in terms of managing people and self and
time, but as far as freedom is concerned, it is not in teaching,
[where] everything is the same everyday — the same schedule,

the same bell ringing. Teaching can be a stifling atmosphere. There's not much change in the schools, although there are workshops. It's not a stimulating atmosphere. For some teachers, it's nice because it's a safe atmosphere.

She says that she could not return to the "regime of the public schools." Besides the routine and lack of professional growth in teaching, Vicky also complains about the future earnings in teaching: "Not that money is the ultimate, but I could only go as far as I did in salary and credits." She made $36,000, the top of the salary schedule when she left, but now earns three times as much in her business.

Carl Fisher: "I'm at the low ebb of my career." Carl always thought he would make his career in the navy but discovered after a few years that he could not handle the "nonsense" of military life. He enrolled in college and found that the courses in which he did relatively well, business and science, easily opened the doors to teaching. In the absence of other options, he decided to try it.

The strongest memory Carl has of his first year in the classroom is fear — fear of being unprepared. He had not anticipated the long hours that would be involved. Nor was he prepared for what students were actually like: "I did a lot of adjusting to the students. They didn't fit my stereotype. I thought they'd sit and listen to me." Despite the rude awakening, Carl gradually grew to like teaching.

He has been teaching business and science for 23 years and basically has been satisfied with his job. In the recent past, however, he has become very unhappy and depressed about his work. Carl had previously thought he would wait until he was 60 to retire, but now he thinks he can hang on for only 4 more years until he is 55. He is looking to transfer or leave teaching as soon as he can without forfeiting too much in retirement benefits. For the past 5 years Carl has been at Rolling Hills. He was happier at his previous school, where he recalls teaching an advanced course to students who were a "tremendous bunch — good achievers and hard workers who produced." He felt he was "on a high" with them. Since his move to Rolling Hills, Carl has been assigned to more introductory courses, and he admits to having difficulty controlling and getting work out of the students. The problems range from trivial matters, such as continuous gum chewing, to swearing in class and not doing assignments.

An administrator ranks Carl very low in effectiveness — "a 2 out of 10" — because of his trouble with discipline and the lack of structure in his lessons. When asked how Carl could have survived as a teacher for such a long time with such low ratings, the administrator responded that Carl was probably given better evaluations at his former school even though he was never a "burning educator who lit kids up."

Even before coming to Rolling Hills, Carl had difficulty with discipline and had been directed to a course in class management. More significantly, the financial situation in the district had recently changed. Whereas Carl had primarily taught business at his old school, he was now required to teach more science at Rolling Hills. Due to the cutbacks in the district, an administrator explained, each faculty member now teaches in a critical area, and Carl's weaknesses, tolerated in earlier years, have become more visible and problematic not only to the administration but to fellow faculty, who express resentment about having him in their department.

Colleagues volunteered how frustrating it was to remediate students after they had had Carl. Often seen eating alone in the noisy faculty lunchroom, Carl reveals that he feels "isolated" among his colleagues, whom he considers "cliquish."

From Carl's perspective, his career has, until recently, been fairly rewarding, providing him with some personal satisfactions: "When you finally get kids to learn something, you feel good about it." To him, his problems have to do with the change in the kind of student he now has, although he admits that he has changed as well. He recalls that many things on the job did not bother him when he was younger, but now he is less inclined to want to "put up with the hassle."

Carl also mentions "the continuous annoyances—the little things that never get solved." An example of one of those problems: Carl contacted a parent about a student's not doing work, and the parent laid the blame on Carl. The lack of administrative support for discipline is another source of stress. Carl feels stronger backing should be given to the teacher when students are sent to the office for disrupting the class. Smoking nervously, he describes the cumulative effect this has had on his health:

> I'm at the low ebb of my career. It's to the point of being depressing. I'll need to get out. I have a physical problem. My hearing's going. My blood pressure's higher than it should be. I'm tired. Vacations aren't long enough anymore.

As a result, Carl is looking forward to leaving the profession for work that is more physical than mental.

SUMMARY

Rolling Hills High School is a pleasure for most to teach in. Not only does it have an academically motivated and capable student body, it also has organizational features that encourage teachers to do their best. The school's policies and practices provide important administrative buffering of the classroom from outside interferences and demands and also supply adequate opportunities for professional stimulation and growth. The Rolling Hills administration also allows a strong teachers' voice in school policy through department heads and union representatives — conditions that reportedly contribute to the high level of satisfaction at the school.

These organizational factors help create a positive psychological climate in which the faculty experience good relations with the administration and with each other. This unusual configuration of enabling features was insufficient, however, to buffer certain teachers, particularly in elective fields, from the effects of shrinking financial resources and changing curricular policy at the state level.

CHAPTER 4

Teaching in a Working-Class Community: Roosevelt High School

Before coming to Roosevelt, math teacher Barbara Johnson taught in a ghetto school where she witnessed an 11-year-old fire a gun at another student; she also taught in an affluent public school where she had to deal with rich students who were "spoiled with no discipline." She welcomed the transfer to Roosevelt where things were "normal," with "normal kids, average classes, schedule, and pay." Located in Spring Valley, a suburb of Los Angeles, Roosevelt High School represents a more typical workplace setting than either Rolling Hills or Brown.

Spring Valley is a predominantly white, working-class community whose children generally end up in blue-collar jobs, many in the developing electronics and banking industry nearby. Pick-up trucks and campers dot the front yards of the modest, single-family homes surrounding Roosevelt. In 1986 an average residence with three bedrooms and one and a half baths cost just under $100,000, a relative bargain in California. The average income in the community of 80,000 is about $29,000. This figure is skewed upward by an increasing, although still small, number of professionals and skilled technicians who are attracted by Spring Valley's relatively reasonable prices and safe, low-crime reputation; these newcomers live closer to the interstate freeway in recently constructed homes that provide a wealthier clientele with more privacy and space.

Roosevelt, one of three high schools in the district, is located in the midst of a residential tract, but, fortunately for the students, it is only a quick stroll to Harry's fast-food place, much preferred over the cafeteria. Built in the late 1960s, Roosevelt's windowless, air-conditioned bungalows could easily be mistaken for temporary structures. The spacious, unlittered campus stretches out to include track and football fields and a student parking lot. A permanent billboard at the main entrance announces the upcoming football game. Grassy areas alternate among the low-lying buildings joined to each other by open-air sidewalks. This configuration of buildings allows for multiple points of access to campus and makes it impossible to monitor the comings and goings of students.

A quiet, low-keyed man whom teachers characterize as "accessible" and "nonauthoritarian," Dr. Fred Jones has been principal at Roosevelt for 3 years. Plaques of appreciation from student groups and pictures of sports teams line his office walls. Dr. Jones is strongly committed to staff development, an area in which he has had a special interest since his research experience in graduate school. In contrast to Brown's principal, Horace Anderson, who maintains a visible profile around school and seldom leaves campus, Fred Jones delegates more responsibilities to his assistant principals and is called off campus for district business several times a week.

According to administrators, teachers in this district would welcome a transfer to Roosevelt; they regard it as a good place to work. The faculty consists of 84 teachers, 98% of whom are white and half of whom have been with the school since its opening 20 years ago. On paper, Roosevelt resembles Rolling Hills High School; at both schools the size and ethnic makeup of the student body and faculty are remarkably similar. In other ways, Roosevelt feels more like Brown, sharing similar struggles with high student absences and apathy. In terms of career outcomes, however, Roosevelt falls between the high-socioeconomic-status school and the poorer inner-city school, offering a useful midpoint for study.

COMMUNITY CHARACTERISTICS:
STUDENT COMPOSITION AND ACHIEVEMENT

Roosevelt has a student body of 1,950 in grades 10 through 12. According to the California Achievement Program, Roosevelt's students score at approximately the 60th percentile in reading and math. Seven hundred students enter Roosevelt's 10th grade; generally about 550 of those will make it through 12th-grade graduation, an attrition of about 150 students. The exact dropout rate is unknown. Site administrators believe that most of the dropouts eventually register at continuation or adult schools; some transfer to other high schools. Table 4.1 summarizes the school's major characteristics.

Although many functions at the school are computerized and terminals occupy the desks of the principal, his assistants, and the counselors, the equipment has not been put to use in tracking students after

TABLE 4.1. Summary of School Characteristics, Roosevelt High School

Location: Los Angeles suburb
Grades: 10-12
Number of teachers employed full time: 84
Average class size: 32
Number of students enrolled in September 1986: 1,950
Ethnicity of students: 8% Hispanic & Asian; 92% white
Ethnicity of faculty: 98% white
Student socioeconomic status: working class; 2% qualify for state welfare
Daily student absences: 17-23%
Dropout rates: 20% of 10th graders

graduation; the information on what students do after graduation is sketchy — a contrast to the informative records maintained at Rolling Hills and Brown. Estimates of the numbers of students who go on to 4-year colleges vary from 7% to 20%, depending on the administrator. Estimates of the portion of the graduating class who attend 2-year colleges range between 30% and 40%. Roughly half the students continue on to some form of higher education.

The student body is racially quite homogeneous: 92% are white, with Hispanics and Southeast Asian students comprising the remaining 8%. Only 1% of the students are identified as having limited English and requiring special language help. Few families (2%) qualify for state welfare. In terms of the homogeneity of student needs, Roosevelt is much more like Rolling Hills than like Brown. The majority of Roosevelt's teachers (53%) do not have any classes predominantly filled with students requiring remedial help.

Roosevelt is remarkably similar to Brown, however, in terms of student apathy and absences. At Brown, absences range from 16% to 18%; Roosevelt estimates are slightly higher, running between 17% and 23%. Parents and teachers at Roosevelt feel helpless in the face of this problem. Most students come from homes in which both parents work or from single-parent homes. Many students congregate at the park or just stay at home during the day, and working parents are unable to monitor the situation. One teacher complains dejectedly about his students, who rest their tennis shoes up on their desks and talk to each other throughout class: "Far too few students have a desire to learn or even attend school." Yet, in comparison with Brown, Roosevelt has more students who achieve academically.

Student apathy or alienation from school has long been a problem at Roosevelt, and the administration has tried various strategies to alleviate it. Several years ago, the administration initiated a career program aimed at strengthening the connection between student interests and academics in order to increase student motivation in the classroom. The career program, still in the process of development, has met with some success, but the high level of absences persists. Attendance is especially problematic after lunch and in the spring, during the warm southern California beach weather. Recently, the principal shortened the lunch period to half an hour in the hopes of discouraging students from leaving campus and skipping their afternoon classes. Also, the school has recently implemented a student incentive system, whereby students with good attendance for a week qualify to take part in a lottery for prizes.

WORKLOAD AND SOURCES OF STRESS

The student-teacher ratio (about 32 : 1) is nearly identical to that at the other two schools. The loudest and most frequent complaint from Roosevelt faculty, however, is aimed at the lack of support for discipline. At Roosevelt, this primarily involves how to deal with poor attendance, a situation requiring teachers to "continually back-up" and slow down for students who do attend. Fletcher Drake, a competent social studies teacher with 24 years of classroom experience, discussed his frustration with student absences that occasionally run as high as one-third of the class: "[I think my classroom effectiveness is] generally good, *if* kids show up. I can't teach kids if they're not here. If allowed to teach, I can get the kids to learn."

For most teachers, the primary frustration is not with the students but with the lack of support from the administration. Brad King, a highly regarded science teacher, exemplified this perspective: "The only problems I feel I have are not with the kids, it's with the administration — their condoning kids being out of class [by not enforcing stricter attendance rules]. . . ."

Roy Davis, an effective science teacher, elaborated on the kind of administrative support that would help teachers do their best in the classroom but is lacking at Roosevelt:

I see a breakdown of discipline and enforcement of attendance [at Roosevelt]. There has to be strong support of classroom teachers and effective discipline. There's lots of room for improvement here. It's useful to have a system where students feel it's important to be in class. Students aren't challenged [criticized] when they miss class. There's a high absence rate. Each day's valuable [in my class], and I have things scheduled that are difficult to make up.

The concern about the lack of administrative support for discipline runs so high among Roosevelt's faculty that only 22% of them indicated they felt the support was adequate, a much lower figure than at either Brown (where 73% of the faculty were satisfied) or at Rolling Hills (where 67% expressed satisfaction). The comparison with Brown is significant since, despite the pressures on disciplinary order that are greater in the inner city, Brown's faculty is satisfied that the administration has done its best given the circumstances. Roosevelt's faculty does not share that confidence in its administration. A contributory factor to Roosevelt's high student absences is the open arrangement of buildings on a campus bounded by roads. This physical configuration allows easy exit and prohibits the close monitoring of students that is possible in Brown's sole building or at Rolling Hills, where the campus is geographically closed off.

The absence of parental support for discipline is also a significant source of stress and frustration. Susan Miller, a home economics teacher looking forward to an early retirement, complained bitterly about belligerent parents who blame teachers for student failure due to incomplete assignments and absences. Only a small proportion of the faculty (19%) is satisfied with parental support, a situation more similar to Brown (where only 7% are satisfied) than to Rolling Hills (where 78% declare their satisfaction).

Despite the absences, certainly a major impediment to effectiveness, Roosevelt teachers generally feel efficacious and successful in their work, resembling Rolling Hills' teachers more than Brown's in this respect. Special education teacher Gwen Sanchez captured her colleagues' sentiments when she declared: "I enjoy teaching and think I'm very effective." The majority of the Roosevelt teachers (70%) judged that they had met their instructional goals with more than 60% of their students (compared with 90% of the teachers at Rolling Hills and 33% of them at Brown). Moreover, nearly half (46%) of Roosevelt's faculty felt "very effective" in getting their students to learn (compared with 56% at Rolling Hills and 26% at Brown). Table 4.2 compares the sense of efficacy across the three schools.

TABLE 4.2. Sense of Efficacy Across Schools (Survey Data, N = 215)

Percentage of faculty who:	Brown (n = 101)	Roosevelt (n = 59)	Rolling Hills (n = 55)
Feel "very effective" in getting students to learn	26%	46%	56%
Accomplished their instructional goals with over 60% of their students	33%	70%	90%

DISTRICT- AND STATE-LEVEL INFLUENCES: PROFESSIONAL CONCERNS

A sense of powerlessness and alienation from the district administration runs through the interviews with the Roosevelt teachers. Comments such as "we have a factory model of industrial relations" in the district or "teachers are treated like the lowest cog in a machine" illustrate the faculty's frustration with district administrators "who have never been in the classroom to see what's going on." A teacher responding to one student's complaint in a class said: "I don't make the rules. I just work here."

A foreign language teacher argued for a more professional role for teachers through participation in policy making: "I want input and participation [in policies]. We let ourselves be treated like little workers and go against sound educational ideas."

Teachers draw a distinction between their satisfaction with the school site administration and their satisfaction with the district administration. They expressed dissatisfaction with the management at the district level and the constraints placed on the school's management. Stan Henry, an industrial arts teacher for more than 20 years, explained how the district's policies and actions undermine school site effectiveness and control:

> The biggest problem [at Roosevelt] is the attendance. The school has done as much as it could. The district has changed its mind [about attendance policy]. If parents raise Cain, this is a spineless district.
>
> Attendance problems can't be left only to the local site. The district is only interested in the ADA [average daily attendance—figures that generate money from the state]. For exam-

ple, if kids miss "x" number of days, they're allowed back in school, even if they haven't been sick. Kids can beat the system. There's no punishment for missing school.

Mark Hanson, a mentor teacher in business education, clarified how district policy has a direct impact on his classes:

At the district level, we have little control over our area. Input needs to be considered. One [district] decision could have devastated our department. I was very frustrated.

I became a mentor teacher so that I could have a chance to have some influence. I now have access to district people and share proposals with them. Things are changing so rapidly [in curriculum] that we have to safeguard our area.

At Roosevelt, state-level changes influenced career attitudes in the same way they affected faculty at Rolling Hills. Proposition 13, which drastically cut funds for education in California, translated into reductions in program quality and increasing pressure on teachers in elective programs to teach in their minor subject areas. Bernard Norris, a former music teacher, quit because he saw "the writing on the wall" after Proposition 13 and was unwilling to make the predicted cuts and compromises in the quality of his music program.

State and district policies had an adverse effect on classroom effectiveness through what teachers perceived as unrealistic or inappropriate curriculum guidelines. Diane Jacobs, an outstanding foreign language teacher, recounted how this is a source of stress for her: "[Because of curriculum guidelines from the district and state,] we have to cover certain content at certain levels. I'm pressured and hassled for time. I feel strangled by the pace."

Weak mechanisms for teachers' input contribute to the powerlessness they experience. The teachers rarely referred to union activities as part of their lives or the life of the school. Department chairs, who perform an advocacy role for teachers at Rolling Hills, are weakened at Roosevelt by the absence of incentives: no extra pay or release time is allotted to those willing to take up the extra responsibilities. In the science department, these responsibilities are now spread among its faculty. In other departments, the energy the chair invests in the job depends on individual goodwill rather than structural incentives. Consequently, leadership for faculty and curriculum concerns is diluted.

PROFESSIONAL GROWTH AND INVOLVEMENT

A veteran English teacher nearing retirement observed that professional development opportunities are much better since Dr. Ford arrived. In the past 9 months, she attended four workshops. Several times a year, the school schedules minimum-length days to give the faculty an opportunity to attend in-services. The school also has some discretionary money for school improvement from the state that it uses to send faculty to conferences.

The teachers are generally satisfied with these formal opportunities to grow professionally. More than half of Roosevelt's faculty (56%) indicated that they felt the professional development opportunities were adequate (compared with 67% at Rolling Hills and only 29% at Brown). The relatively rich opportunities at Roosevelt have encouraged more than a third of the faculty (39%) to increase their participation in professional development workshops and courses over the recent years — an indication of continued growth. By contrast, 68% of Rolling Hills' teachers and only 29% of Brown's faculty reported a similar increase.

More than half of the faculties at the three study schools are highly involved, in that they spend over 50 hours a week on their work (57% of the faculty at Roosevelt; 56% at Rolling Hills; and 53% at Brown). At each school, the average number of hours expended on work closely matches the national average of 49 hours per week (N.E.A., 1987). However, these averages mask significant variation among the schools. Very few teachers at Roosevelt and Rolling Hills work only 40 hours or less a week — only 14% at Roosevelt and 11% at Rolling Hills. By contrast, nearly a third of the Brown teachers (32%) reported working the minimum hours. This high proportion can be explained partially by the numerous time-compensated positions at Brown that give many teachers reduced teaching loads. Table 4.3 displays the differences in workload across the schools.

COLLEGIAL EXCHANGE AND PEER INTERACTION

If the faculty lunchroom is a barometer of the level of collegiality, things are at a low ebb at Roosevelt. At noon, the large faculty lunchroom adjacent to the student cafeteria is nearly empty save for a single round table of regulars. For some time, a second table has been set up in the unlikely event that more teachers will arrive; the other tables are folded and pushed here and there against the blank walls, creating the inaccurate impression of a temporary arrangement. Some faculty mem-

TABLE 4.3. Comparison of Workload Across Schools
(Survey Data, *N* = 215)

Percentage of faculty who:	Brown (*n* = 101)	Roosevelt (*n* = 59)	Rolling Hills (*n* = 55)
Spend over 50 hours/week on school work	53%	57%	56%
Spend 40 or fewer hours/week on school work	32%	14%	11%
Teach 5 periods/day	57%	81%	91%
Have 3 to 5 classes with predominantly remedial students	49%	19%	21%

bers spend their short half-hour lunch period in the small faculty mailroom, others in the even smaller department offices or in their classrooms.

The dispersion at noon is symptomatic of the departmentalization and lack of unity among the faculty. Fred Dixon, a friendly man who is active in the union, offered a personal example of the fragmentation among the staff:

> I don't interact much with other departments. . . . There's not a lot of unity among the faculty. We're fragmented, not cohesive. There are 15 new faculty [this year], and I know only a third.

Roosevelt's psychological climate is affected by the chronic complaints of a large portion of the faculty. Many Roosevelt teachers (42%) believe that the colleagues they frequently interact with are dissatisfied with teaching (a proportion much closer to Brown's 51% than to Rolling Hills' 8%). An outstanding teacher observed that half of the teachers in her department are dissatisfied with their jobs and repeat the same things in their classes. Her strategy to avoid becoming like the complainers is to consciously avoid the negative people and to "pick out friends with the same goals who are good teachers and like kids."

Although the faculty has frequent opportunities for formal in-services and workshops, teachers have few opportunities for collegial exchange at the department or school level. A mentor teacher spoke of the great value of "observing other teachers and seeing how they do it" for gaining new ideas and giving each other feedback. He bemoaned the rarity of this kind of collegial interaction due to the lack of administrative arrangements and support. Ironically, he has to attend conferences off campus to see teachers in action; unfortunately, these teachers are not his Roosevelt colleagues.

Although the school has a good reputation among teachers throughout the district, only 53% of the faculty report satisfaction with teaching at Roosevelt, a proportion that is more similar to responses from Brown in the inner city than from Rolling Hills in the suburbs. While many teachers agree that Roosevelt is "an above average school," nearly half of the faculty are dissatisfied with it as a workplace. Table 4.4 compares the levels of teacher satisfaction across the schools.

TEACHING CAREERS AT ROOSEVELT HIGH SCHOOL

Despite the significant proportion of the teachers who are dissatisfied with teaching at Roosevelt, 72% of the faculty indicate satisfaction with teaching as a job (a much higher proportion than Brown's 54%, but not as high as Rolling Hills' 81%).

Over the next 5 years, about 12% of Roosevelt's faculty are likely to quit. Another 14% indicate that they are undecided about staying in or leaving the profession. (An additional 19% of the faculty are likely to

TABLE 4.4. Comparison of Teacher Satisfaction Across Schools (Survey Data, $N = 215$)

Percentage of faculty who:	Brown ($n = 101$)	Roosevelt ($n = 59$)	Rolling Hills ($n = 55$)
Are satisfied with teaching as a job	54%	72%	81%
Are satisfied with teaching at their school	54%	53%	89%
Rate close colleagues as satisfied with teaching	32%	39%	74%
Rate close colleagues as dissatisfied with teaching	51%	42%	8%
Are satisfied with administrative support for discipline	73%	22%	67%
Are satisfied with parental support	7%	19%	78%
Are satisfied with opportunities for professional growth	29%	56%	67%
Are satisfied with the adequacy of class materials	44%	41%	46%

retire.) These percentages place Roosevelt between the other two schools in terms of career decisions to defect. Coupled with earlier data on job attitudes, these figures reveal a unique pattern of career outcomes at each school. Table 4.5 illustrates the differences in teachers' career intentions among the schools.

An inspection of the list of Roosevelt's interviewees reveals a predominance of good-fit teachers, a contrast to the high proportion of weak-fit teachers at Brown. Although Roosevelt's faculty were affected by identical environmental forces at the state level as Rolling Hills' faculty, Roosevelt's leavers represent a broader cross-section of subject areas and are not drawn primarily from the nonacademic areas as they are at Rolling Hills. Table 4.6 lists major characteristics of all the Roosevelt teachers who were interviewed.

Good-Fit Stayers

Diane Jacobs: "I still love teaching." Diane Jacobs is a self-confident, energetic foreign language teacher and department chair at Roosevelt. She recalls knowing early on—from the ninth grade—that she would become a teacher. Her older sister taught, and Diane had several teachers who were good models and encouraged her to teach. She also loved French and felt there was not much she could do with the language except teach it. So she became a teacher. When she first entered teaching, however, Diane was uncertain how long she would remain in the classroom. Like other women with spiral careers, she expected to leave teaching to raise a family and possibly return to it much later.

TABLE 4.5. Comparison of Future Career Plans Across Schools (Survey Data, *N* = 215)

Percentage of faculty who:	Brown (*n* = 101)	Roosevelt (*n* = 59)	Rolling Hills (*n* = 55)
Will likely leave teaching in 5 years (excludes retirees)	18%	12%	6%
Are undecided about whether they will stay or leave (excludes retirees)	15%	14%	7%
Will likely stay in teaching in the next 5 years (excludes retirees)	48%	56%	56%
Will likely retire in the next 5 years	20%	19%	31%

TABLE 4.6. Interviewees' Characteristics, Roosevelt High School (*n* = 24)

Name	Age	Years in Teaching	Subject Taught	Hours Worked Weekly	Supervisor Evaluation
GOOD-FIT STAYERS					
Diane Jacobs*	38	16	French	48	10
Fletcher Drake	48	24	Social Studies	52	6.5
Fred Dixon	42	20	Social Studies	42	3
Lester Samuels	39	1	Business	51	7
Brenda Ring*	27	6	English	41	8
GOOD-FIT UNDECIDEDS					
Jackie Paul*	40	12	English	54	9
Faye Smythe*	23	1	English	51	7
Barbara Johnson	31	10	Math	50	10
GOOD-FIT LEAVERS					
Susan Miller*	51	19	Home Economics	39	7
Stan Henry	48	22	Industrial Arts	45	6.5
Rob Bole*	38	16	English	39	3
Doris Ryan	45	20	Science	42	5
Steve Ross†	37	14	English	40	4
Bernard Norris†	33	7	Music	64	7.5
Lisa Cross†	30	10	Special Ed.	58	8
Harry Dover†	40	18	Math	40	3
Russell Simon†	40	15	Math	45	2
WEAK-FIT STAYERS					
Sara Howard	50	18	English	50	7.5
Mark Hanson	42	17	Business	47	9.5
Brad King	42	16	Science	47	9.5
Roy Davis	40	18	Science	56	8
WEAK-FIT UNDECIDEDS					
Gwen Sanchez	30	5	Special Ed.	34	10
WEAK-FIT LEAVERS					
Laura Andrews	50	17	Math	45	9
Martin Barnes*	30	6	PE/Math/Coaching	57	7

*The interview with this teacher is included as a vignette.

†This teacher has already left the profession.

Notes: (1) Teachers who say they will quit teaching before they reach 55 years of age and before qualifying for full retirement benefits are considered leavers; teachers who say they will stay in teaching for 5 years but are not sure after that are considered "undecideds."

(2) In the first round of interviews at Roosevelt, I did not have enough representation in some subject areas or of the younger teachers, so I added a few more teachers. Thus the sample of interviewees is slightly larger at this school.

Married soon after college, she moved to California, where her husband was offered a good job. Her first position was in 1967, teaching seventh grade, and she has fond memories of that period. At first she felt alone and frightened, but she developed a critical relationship with Mrs. Peters, a veteran teacher at the school, whom Diane refers to as a "mentor," "protector," and "mother-figure." During preparation periods, Diane observed Mrs. Peters and spent time later with her talking about the class. They spent considerable time together developing plans and discussing methodology, and Diane credits Mrs. Peters with teaching her how to teach, especially the difficult areas of oral proficiency and pronunciation. Diane refers to Mrs. Peters as her "professional friend" who helped her gain self-confidence and got her off to a running start as a good teacher.

After a few years, she took a leave to have a baby. Six months later, realizing she was bored at home, she returned to teaching. But by her seventh year in the classroom, she had reached what she saw as her "stagnation point" and remembers feeling "burned out":

> I got tired of doing the same old thing—not growing professionally. I had no place to go—only into administration, but I didn't want to go there, [because] I wouldn't be good at telling other people what to do. I asked myself: "Five or 20 years down the road, would I be happy doing this teaching the rest of my life?"

Seeking to quell her doubts about teaching, Diane decided to take a sabbatical to enroll in college courses and to put together a new curriculum in the hopes of revitalizing her involvement in the classroom. At the same time she thought about job alternatives. She seriously considered going to law school, but weighed that against the demands on her family life and decided against it. She recalls:

> My husband said I had to do whatever would make me happy, but I should take a good look at trying something else. [As a teacher] I had my summers free and was home in the afternoon. He said, "Are you willing to find yourself with crazy hours with a new job? What about us [the family]?" My students, when they heard I might leave, said, "What do you mean [that you might leave]!" They were horrified. All things considered—my lifestyle and free time—it wasn't worth it to plunge into something else.

Because of her strong family values, the occupational benefits of teaching were a strong incentive to stay. But vacations and free time were not the only factors keeping her in teaching. After her sabbatical, she became involved in cooperative learning, which radically changed her method of teaching. It was this innovative approach — and, ironically, not the courses developed during her sabbatical — that gave her what she called her "fresh start" in teaching. An administrator had asked her to be a faculty representative in a partnership program with a university. Diane agreed because she was still searching for something to give her new energy. She started meeting on a regular basis with other teachers, and a cooperative learning model developed from that collaboration. Today she uses this method in her own classes and plays a leadership role in training other teachers in the district.

When offered the chance to get an administrative credential, Diane rejected that opportunity. She wanted to continue working with students, something she did well: "[Becoming an administrator] doesn't appeal to me — being in an office and shuffling papers. My main enjoyment is contact with kids. That's what I do best."

Diane's notion of career advancement has to do with progress in a professional sense. Specifically, a teaching career for Diane means professional growth — "learning new things, new approaches, meeting with colleagues, and being part of decision making which affects my classroom — decisions about policy and curriculum." To Diane, important reasons for staying in teaching have to do with opportunities that keep her vital and fresh as a teacher and the power to participate in decisions that directly affect her work. Organizational factors, such as having supportive administrators who provide release time for training and who solicit her opinion, are crucial to providing the opportunity and power so important to Diane.

Diane's master plan is to retire at age 55 and then to travel with her husband, who is an engineer. Her primary reason for staying in teaching is the satisfaction she receives from helping her students learn: "I love my kids." After 16 years in the classroom, she speaks enthusiastically about her work: "I still love teaching. I like working with young people [and] watching them learn" — a common statement from good-fit teachers who have decided to stay. Recently chosen to be a mentor teacher, Diane is referred to by her peers and administrators as "an outstanding teacher."

The intrinsic rewards from teaching — from being able to teach well — are at the heart of her decision to stay in the profession until retirement. Being in a school that allows her to be successful and inventive in the classroom enables her to secure those rewards.

At the same time, Diane's age has some effect on the high probability of her staying in teaching. In her late thirties, she feels "programmed" into teaching, never having trained for anything else. She is at a point in her life when it would be harder to switch jobs than when she originally contemplated doing so 10 years ago. Diane adds that she likes teaching because she is "security-minded," and teaching has a great deal of job security, so much so that she would have to "pop nude out of a cake" before she would be fired. Another significant factor in her decision to stay is the free time to spend with her family as a result of the school calendar. Overall, she believes that teaching suits her quite well.

Diane, then, is primarily drawn to teaching by its intrinsic rewards, but as a middle-aged woman with a family, she also finds the security and fit with her personal life attractive.

Brenda Ring: "I have found my niche in life with teaching." An English teacher in her late twenties, Brenda Ring has been teaching for 6 years. Brenda, whose boyfriend also teaches, is evaluated by a Roosevelt administrator as an effective teacher. She foresees remaining in the classroom for a long time, possibly moving into counseling later in her career because she enjoys getting to know the students personally, something she finds impossible with 30 students in a class. At the same time she is reluctant to leave the regular classroom because she believes, "If I can make 30 kids enjoy English, I am happy. I've found my niche in life with teaching."

Brenda's early years were not unlike those of many other new recruits who entered into a tight job market for teachers. She had only a temporary contract during her first semester. For the second semester she was offered a position teaching art. She rejected the offer, which would have given her another temporary contract, and opted for a less secure position as a day-to-day substitute because she felt insecure teaching out of her subject area: "I want to be good at what I do, so I said 'no' and [instead] got my girlfriend who is in art to do the job." Her persistence and good work eventually got her hired as a long-term substitute that year. During her second year she was given a temporary contract. A regular contract position finally became available in her fifth year. Despite the uncertainty of whether or not she would be rehired each year, she persisted in teaching.

Brenda works with many students needing remedial help, a task she finds extremely frustrating:

> I see kids who aren't going to make it — kids who don't see the connection between succeeding in school and succeeding in life. I find out things about students and am sad about their

personal life, their situation with their parents, [and] how they've been dealt bad cards in life.

Despite the frustrations of working with high need students, Brenda enjoys her work because she feels she makes a difference and because she can be creative:

> I like kids who are having a tough time because I can do some good and make them feel good about themselves even though they may not learn much about the subject.
>
> I feel good about what I do. I enjoy 30 different personalities each hour. I see kids feel good about things they do. I can get kids to respond. I have a lot of leeway with what I can do in class. It stirs my creativity to come up with assignments. Because I teach English, I get the kids to write journals and so I really get to know them.

Her affinity for students with special needs comes from her own school experience, which she describes as boring. Many of her intellectually capable friends dropped out of school. She also recalls that her ninth-grade counselor predicted a need for teachers.

Brenda's primary reason to stay in teaching stems from her work with students and their feedback: "Kids like my teaching. They think it's fun and I get a positive evaluation from them. I also get a positive evaluation from the administration. They say I have good control and rapport with the students." The recognition she receives from her students and the administration are a source of great personal satisfaction and a major factor in her decision to stay in teaching. Another reason is that in her opinion "the pay is good." She presently makes $21,600.

Good-Fit Undecideds

Faye Smythe: "I've come through the toughest experience of my life." In her early twenties, Faye Smythe has completed the first semester of her first year of full-time teaching. She teaches three American history classes and two civics courses at Roosevelt. According to an administrator, Faye is doing very well as a beginning teacher and rates as "a 7 out of 10" in effectiveness. Despite the good evaluation, Faye is undecided about her future in teaching. She entered teaching for several reasons. Her primary motivation was to work in what she called "a helping profession," a commitment derived from her strong Christian beliefs. She also chose teaching because her husband first became a teacher and she was intrigued by what he did. So she enrolled in an education course, and that led to other courses and a teaching credential. In addition, Faye values her time with her husband, so the summers off, coupled with her desire to help others, made teaching seem like a good choice.

This first year has been extremely frustrating because she has not been as successful as she wants to be, a typical concern of beginning teachers:

> I've come through the toughest experience of my life. I'm not satisfied with being very good. I'm a perfectionist, and that puts added pressure on me. I'm not satisfied with my work this semester. I haven't done a bad job, but I haven't been outstanding either.
>
> I compare myself to other teachers. Why can't I be like that? Other teachers do awesome things. They get everybody involved in group activities. I haven't been able to see many teachers, but some can get to higher-level thinking skills. I'd like to be there, but can't figure out how to.

Faye considers herself fairly lucky to have only three different preparations and no remedial classes during her first year. Yet the seemingly endless nature of the work, particularly correction of papers, is a major source of stress:

> Teaching is a high-stress job now. It'll lessen as the years go by, [but now] there's a constant workload and 8 hours of work [always] sitting at home for you. There's an unlimited amount you can do for students.
>
> I can't leave the job at school [when I go home at night]. There's constant pressure to correct papers and do lesson plans. I've considered freelance journalism and have written some articles. I want to get away from the high stress of this job. You could work 7 days a week, 24 hours a day, and you need to draw a line. I'm still trying to figure out where to draw the line.

The incessant demands on her time provoke Faye, who works more than 50 hours a week, to actively consider leaving the teaching profession. Discipline, class size, and attendance problems are other important workload issues:

> I'm not by nature somebody who likes to tell others what to do. I have no outward problem with discipline, but sometimes I

feel like a witch at the end of the day. I'm constantly nagging them and want them to do what's right. They need to see from day one that you mean business.

Classroom behavior is okay in most of the classes, but in one class I have to tell them to be quiet and lower the level of the class. I like working with students one to one, and I like the education field, but facing 30 kids is overwhelming.

[Also] the number of absences and tardies is a problem. It's not unusual for one-third of the class to be gone. Sometimes when it's a nice beach day, half of the students are absent. It's hard for me to accept.

Although Faye thinks that there is a good chance she might leave teaching in the near future, some inducements hold her in the classroom. Her work with students does yield some measure of satisfaction: "I like seeing students learn, [for example] when they understand new concepts. I like to watch them grow in ideas."

Still another source of satisfaction is the informal collegial interaction and support:

I enjoy the staff. Other staff members give me ideas and are very supportive. They share their dittos with me. I [also] have conversations with teachers in the faculty room and get informal help that way. For example, I'm teaching the Civil War, and a teacher volunteered to send over a bunch of materials they had used. These informal conversations are the most helpful [to my learning how to teach].

The hours and vacations, well-suited to the demands of raising a family, have acquired increasing importance in Faye's career deliberations. Her future responsibilities as a mother are very important to her, and teaching would allow her to carry out those responsibilities reasonably well. Her plans are to have children in a few years. A possible scenario would be to leave teaching for several years and come back later, perhaps on a part-time basis, so she could devote more time to her family:

After I have kids and they're in school, it's somewhat likely I would return to teaching. I'd definitely stay home with them until they're in school. Then after that I'd like to work part time because teaching social studies is so time consuming. Or I could work part time in a private school or tutor.

The salary is another attractive feature of teaching. According to Faye, "It's a professional pay compared to other jobs."

Jackie Paul: "I am seriously considering another job, although I don't want to." Unlike most undecided teachers, Jackie Paul has 12 years of teaching experience, most of it in private schools. A long-term substitute at Roosevelt for the past 2 years, she is seriously considering leaving the teaching profession. Rated by her supervisor as an "excellent" English teacher, Jackie entered teaching because she wanted to work with people. She knew in the eighth grade that she would be a teacher; she was so moved watching a teacher conduct a lesson on Shakespeare that she told herself, "That's what I want to do!" Like Faye, Jackie also credits her strong religious belief as a major factor in her choice of professions: "It's God's plan for me [to teach] and I've never regretted it."

She recalls her first year in teaching at a private school as "a great year with a strong staff" and attributes her early sense of success to a strong mentor relationship with a more experienced teacher:

> I felt positive after the first year — that I had been a success and students had learned. I had Mrs. Samuels and we talked about ideas all the time. I was trying my wings as a teacher and the students were agreeable. It was a very positive year.

Jackie transferred from a private school to Roosevelt 2 years ago when her husband found a job in the area as a school administrator. But the district did not give her credit for her previous classroom experience and started her as a daily substitute making $53 a day. Subsequently, she was given a raise to $74 a day as a long-term substitute, equivalent to a modest annual salary of less than $15,000, about $5,000 less than a beginning teacher on a regular contract. During her first year at Roosevelt, she was instrumental in securing a grant for a computer lab at the school. Yet, despite her extra effort and excellent evaluation, the district did not offer her a regular contract or salary at the end of the year. Jackie, who spends at least 54 hours a week on her work, resents being paid less than more inexperienced teachers.

She is enthusiastic, however, about the work itself and feels successful: "I love teaching. I don't even mind doing grades. With the majority of kids, I'm very effective. I can see them learning. I know my goals and the class gets them."

Jackie also likes the school, even though poor attendance and tardiness are a problem. She believes she receives adequate support from the administration in disciplinary matters, contrasting working at Roosevelt to her last experience at an elite private school with "spoiled rich kids" where teachers received no support from the administrators.

Other workplace arrangements make teaching stimulating. This year Jackie attended a writing conference and four computer workshops. Appreciative of the availability of many such opportunities at Roosevelt, she also values the freedom to write grants and to try new things, such as using computers to teach writing.

Despite her satisfaction with the workplace, Jackie is undecided about her commitment to stay in teaching and is reluctantly considering other jobs. Unlike most other teachers interviewed, her reasons hinge on money:

> I've felt like leaving in the last 2 years more than ever before. For personal and financial reasons. I came to this school with 10 years of experience, and they didn't give me any credit for those years. I'm overqualified, and that's a sore spot.
>
> Also, the family's growing up. I have two girls who'll be going to college. It costs a lot to live — piano lessons, orthodontists. . . . [She smiles.] I put in an application for a job after school at a department store. I'm seriously considering another job, although I don't want to.

Although Jackie likes teaching at Roosevelt, her commitment to teaching is contingent on being given a regular contract and salary. Anything less is unfair in her eyes and inadequate for her family's needs.

Good-Fit Leavers

Susan Miller: "I'm not the kind of teacher I used to be." Susan had a rocky beginning teaching at her first school and quit after the first year. She felt marginally successful and became disenchanted with teaching after her principal criticized her for speaking out about school policy. After her two children were born, her husband went to law school, and she reluctantly started substitute teaching at Roosevelt to help pay the bills. But she found the environment so much better at Roosevelt than at her first placement that she accepted a permanent position. At her new school she finally felt free to express herself, even to be critical. During her years at Roosevelt, she also appreciated the freedom to create new courses in her field, and until recently, when the state money for vocational education decreased, she thought that the opportunities were quite good for professional growth.

Susan links her changing feelings about her job to shifts in state and district policies. These new policies resulted in a decline in the quality of students and in the importance of her subject area:

> I don't want to sound totally negative. The last few years I haven't enjoyed teaching that much. I [do] enjoy it basically, but there are times I don't want to be here any more. It's hard to define my inner feelings. The kind of kids we get might explain things. They're very low academically. My [home ec] classes are a dumping ground. That probably contributes.
>
> Vocational education isn't considered valuable today. I don't think home ec will last very much longer [as a subject]. It's demoralizing. I was sought after and grabbed up [to teach home ec] when I graduated. But Prop[osition] 13 started things going down the tubes. Now Sacramento has decided to push academics. I question if I'm doing anything of real value. Kids who might have taken home ec as an interesting subject don't anymore. The quality [of student in my classes] has gone down.

Susan attributes her problems with discipline and relationships with parents to changes in social attitudes:

> Things have changed in the past 5 years. Half of my time's taken up with discipline, ranging from saying "let's be quiet" to more serious things. Parents have little respect for teachers. I have a student in sixth period who's been absent about 17 times in 11 weeks. I get a call from the mother, who was unbelievably belligerent that I failed her daughter. To the parent it was all my fault. I told her that it was the girl's responsibility to come to me and she didn't. I have about three or four unpleasant encounters with parents a year. Sometimes when attendance is terrible, mothers will even lie for the students.

Demoralized by the attitudes of parents, state policy makers, and district administrators, Susan has decreased her level of effort at work. She admits: "[Although] I'm basically a very good teacher, I'm not the kind of teacher I used to be." She used to enjoy integrating science into her home economics lessons. For example, she brought in cocoons to demonstrate how cloth fibers are made. But she stopped doing extra things because students exhibited an indifference to her efforts by putting their heads down to sleep. Now Susan feels she is "constantly teaching down rather than demanding excellence." When she could take a more academic approach, teaching gave her a personal sense of value and worth. Now she feels guilty for not doing what she was once able to do.

In another year, when her son has graduated from law school and no longer requires her income, Susan is planning to escape from the stress of teaching by becoming a housewife and enjoying jogging on the beach with her dog. Her husband, a lawyer, encouraged her to quit 3 years ago because her acute stress resulted in insomnia. However, she resisted leaving because it made it financially easier for the family to put her son through law school.

Susan works through her lunch and prep period and takes no work home at night. The source of her stress is not primarily the amount of work, but the interaction with a new group of students each hour; each group brings new problems, requiring her to continually switch her approach and thinking. She speaks enviously of a friend, a kindergarten teacher, who has the same group of students the entire day.

Susan cites difficulties in the classroom as one of the main reasons for leaving teaching before full retirement; but she also says that the probability of her subject area being phased out of the curriculum and the devaluation of her specialty are other critical factors. Her demoralization about the profession is reflected in her advice to her son to stay away from teaching because he "could do more with his life" in another occupation.

Rob Bole: "I wasn't getting back enough." Rob Bole desperately wants to leave teaching. He is working on an administrative credential and hopes to escape his English classes in a few years. As a college student Rob decided to become a teacher because he wanted to participate in social change and to be in an intellectually stimulating environment:

> I suppose I always liked education and academic environments. I always liked school — I did well there; although I wasn't exceptional, I got B's and A's. Being a teacher seemed to be a job where I could be involved in social change and be in an academic environment. I like learning and finding out about things. I figured I would always stay in teaching.

Rob began his teaching at Roosevelt High School in the early 1970s and experienced tremendous culture shock. He grew up in an upper-middle-class community where most students went on to college. But in Roosevelt's white working-class setting where most students ended up in blue-collar jobs, school was not what he expected. Kids used to laugh at his college loafers.

His first year was hard. Everything was new, and like many new teachers, Rob received minimal help from his peers and administrators. They told him: "Here are your books. Good luck." Left to his own devices, Rob ended up having to create much of his own material. He remembers completing that first year with a sense of dissatisfaction but also with an optimism that things would improve:

> In retrospect, what I got back from the students [that first year] wasn't a great deal. But I was so busy and idealistic. I told myself, "I'll get to them [i.e., the kids who didn't want to be in school and were apathetic]. Those are problems, but I'll solve them."

Frustrated by students' attitudes, he came to realize that he really wanted to teach kids like himself. "[I was fed up with] working hard, struggling on a daily basis to get cooperation, facing unacceptable attitudes, like 'I hate school,' 'I don't want to do this,' 'Why do I have to do this?'"

In his third year of teaching, he tried to transfer to a wealthier school district, but failed. By his tenth year in the classroom, he started thinking about leaving teaching entirely. He says he was "disillusioned" because teaching had not turned out to be what he had hoped. Five years later, he started to plan for his exit from the profession by enrolling in graduate school to get an administrative credential. He refers to his 15th year as the "worst year" he had ever had: "students were the worst" and there were "lots of discipline problems and lots of uncooperative students."

In earlier years, he thought that he could become accustomed to the dissatisfying conditions or that he might be able to change things. Now he has decided that, although he had had some excellent classes and had done some outstanding things, he "wasn't getting back enough" from his students and he harbored self-doubts about his ability in the classroom:

> It was too much struggle with student attitudes, their not being cooperative, not working, and having poor habits, and not caring about school. I put in a lot of effort to improve instruction. But I had come to a place in my life where I saw that's how they are [and began] doubting my ability to get from them what I want. I want to do a job when I think I can see the

results. I don't want to fight with people to do what they should be doing.

The administration rates Rob as below average in effectiveness. When looking back on his years at Roosevelt, though, Rob recalls receiving little help in his professional development. Although the district and the school sponsor many in-services, he believes that "nothing major" at Roosevelt has helped him become a more effective teacher. In this context, he complains about his sense of isolation and the lack of collegiality among the faculty:

> At this school I haven't gained anything from other teachers. It's pretty departmentalized. Within the department most teachers aren't interested in being collaborative or collegial. They're much older than me — about 8 to 10 years older. There are 10 teachers in my department, some are part-time coaches, so the department isn't very cohesive. The permanent teachers are reluctant to work together. That's one of the things that's really missing [at Roosevelt].

Although Rob received little support from the administration and colleagues, teaching suited him well as a job for many years:

> [Teaching] fits in terms of personal time. I'm organized so that I don't have to prepare at home. I have vacations with my family. I have terrific benefits — thousands [of dollars] a year in medical benefits. And [I have] autonomy — I don't have to answer to anyone.

Yet today Rob has decided to give up teaching because "it has very few rewards, [very little] satisfaction and seeing accomplishments." Given the lack of intrinsic rewards and his low effectiveness, money has become an issue. In his mind, the salary is "bad" primarily because it provides inadequate compensation for his hard work, the lack of student response, and the public perception that teachers are doing a poor job. In Rob's view, his salary is also low in comparison to what his college friends earn. Financial matters mean more to Rob now that he has two children than when he first began teaching. Although he is preparing himself to be a school administrator, he also hopes that work in private industry will be a possibility in the future: "I really want a change. I always have been in schools. Outside the schools is the real world. There might be more opportunity [out] there, although I may be entirely wrong."

Weak-Fit Leaver

   Martin Barnes: "I don't get a lot of positive feedback from kids."
Martin coaches and teaches physical education and math at Roosevelt.
He has been teaching for 6 years but, like Jackie Paul, works under a
temporary contract. Rated a "7 out of 10" in effectiveness, Martin is
working on an administrative credential and hopes to leave the classroom and become a vice-principal within the next few years.
   Martin became a teacher because he loved sports and coaching. He
ended up in the public schools quite by accident, however.

> Becoming a teacher evolved from my desire to coach. I hadn't
> planned to teach before that. I was working for a masters in
> recreation so I could do administration. But the field was clos-
> ing in recreation. There were cutbacks and a glut of people in
> the field. So I got a teaching credential to work at the junior
> college. But I saw the writing on the wall — that community
> college jobs were not going anywhere [and there would be no
> openings].

So when the opportunity arose in the late 1970s to work in a high school
outside of California as a math teacher and football coach, he accepted
it. But he was unhappy during his 2 years there:

> I wasn't happy with the administration. They were fighting
> cutbacks and couldn't support the sports program. I had to
> build the team on my own. No one was on campus to coach
> except for me. I wasn't allowed to fundraise for the team, but I
> didn't have the tools to do a good job. I also saw that teaching
> was unstable. Ten to 12 tenured teachers were laid off while I
> was there.

   Given the instability of the job and his dissatisfaction with the
coaching conditions, Martin left teaching for 2 years. But his experiences on the outside brought him back to education:

> I went into banking, but I didn't like the confinement indoors.
> The pay scale wasn't much better than teaching. As a teacher,
> you can make the same money as a vice-president at a bank. I
> also got a license in insurance, but I learned I'm not a salesper-
> son for knocking on doors.

After being in the real world, you realize that there are trade-offs in any job. I got this job [at Roosevelt] because a friend of mine was head coach here. I came back to teaching with a different approach. I'm goal oriented now. I'm working toward an administrative credential [because] I know this district will have a huge retirement in administration.

His return to the classroom, then, is the result of personal readjustments and new goals rather than a desire to work with students. He explains his reservations about teaching:

I'd like to be a curriculum vice-principal at a high school. It wouldn't bother me to be in the classroom for another 5 years, but I wouldn't do it for 10.

I don't get a lot of positive feedback from kids. It's frustrating if all the kid is interested in is the Friday date. Kids aren't prepared to work. You have to give of yourself to be an effective teacher. That can reach a level which drains the reservoir.

Yet Martin found it worthwhile to return to teaching, despite his lack of enthusiasm for classroom work and ever-present concerns about layoffs. Teaching allows him to gain enough experience to be promoted into administration. Further, one of the attractive trade-offs in teaching is the considerable vacation time that he can spend with his wife and young son. His desire for more responsibility and more pay, however, motivates him to prepare to leave the classroom and enter administration.

SUMMARY

Roosevelt High School, with its "normal kids and average classes," offers unusually rich formal opportunities for professional development and cooperative relations between the site administration and faculty — conditions that make the school "a better than average place to work," according to some teachers. These positive features are qualified by dissatisfaction with the effects of policies at several levels of the educational system. At the school level, the lack of structural support for department chairs weakens leadership among teachers and representation of their concerns; this combined with the sparsity of opportunities for peer exchange contribute to the lack of voice and collegial unity that teachers complain about at Roosevelt. At the district level, the faculty believe they have little input and only weak support for discipline — a condition that reduces their ability to be effective in the classroom. On the state level, economic restrictions and curriculum policies adversely affect job satisfaction and career decisions, especially in certain subject areas.

CHAPTER 5

An Analysis of Careers in Schools

Schools are not equal as places in which to develop a teaching career. The chances of having a satisfying career as a teacher differ markedly at Roosevelt, Brown, and Rolling Hills. Differences in workplace conditions and context contribute to varying levels of job satisfaction, sense of efficacy, and voluntary turnover among teachers. The schools studied here support the conventional wisdom that inner-city conditions produce lower job satisfaction and higher turnover; wealthy suburban conditions result in higher job satisfaction and lower turnover.

These cases, however, also reveal that job satisfaction does not rest simply with teaching wealthy students versus poor ones. The relationship between teachers' job satisfaction and student socioeconomic status is a complex one. Students, the raw material that teachers are given to work with, are the primary component of a school's context (Metz, 1988); they centrally define a teacher's work experience and the parameters of job satisfaction.

From a teacher's perspective, the relevant student characteristic affecting career attitudes and outcomes is educational need:

The homogeneity versus diversity of need, which refers to the number of different handicaps (for example, the variety of language, emotional, motivational, and remedial needs) represented within a single classroom

The level or intensity of need, which is defined as how far behind or advanced students' skills are or how serious the emotional and motivational problems are

These elements affect the level of students' academic achievement as well as how teachers experience their work. As the diversity and intensity of educational need increase, so do teachers' perceptions of workload stress, while sense of effectiveness and satisfaction decline. Class size, although nearly identical at the three sites, elicited different reactions from teachers. Teachers at Rolling Hills who had fairly homogeneous classes seldom mentioned class size as a problem, whereas at

Brown teachers regularly identified this as a serious impediment to effectiveness and satisfaction.

Students' educational needs and academic achievement constitute an important component of the community context of a school. Student characteristics, however, are not the sole determinants of teachers' career attitudes. At each school, environmental factors — community, district, and state characteristics — interact with organizational conditions to mold the total workplace experience. The mutual influence among these workplace factors shapes career attitudes and choice over time.

A strong theme emerging from these diverse cases is the tension between bureaucratic, top-down control and professional discretion. Teachers want schools to be more of "a shared enterprise" — to have more of a collegial and less of an institutional or bureaucratic environment. In addition to wanting more input in policy decisions, teachers at all three schools expressed strong concern about opportunities for growth, collegial interaction, and administrative support to enable classroom effectiveness. These issues derive from common professional concerns about doing one's job well, not merely from desires to make teaching easier or more pleasant. Teachers' interests in more training, the development of competence, and peer interaction are also the same elements necessary for professional identification or bonding (Becker & Carper, 1966).

The interviews and survey data, aggregated by workplace, reveal unique patterns of career attitudes and choice at each school. Within each site, however, variation exists among teachers. The conditions in the same workplace are also individually and differentially experienced. In contrast to the predominant career pattern at each school, Rolling Hills also has dissatisfied teachers who want to leave, Brown has satisfied stayers, and Roosevelt has both very satisfied and very dissatisfied teachers. The personal accounts of teachers' careers illustrate the interaction between personal and workplace factors and the individual processes of career development.

GOOD-FIT STAYERS

"I have found my niche in life with teaching," declared a teacher at Roosevelt with 7 years' experience. "I don't know of anything else I'd rather do," added a veteran teacher at Rolling Hills. These comments are typical of good-fit stayers: teachers who came to the profession with strong motivation and who have chosen to make it their career. These teachers enjoy their interaction with students, want to stay in teaching, and spend considerably more than 40 hours a week on their work. Supervisors generally rate these teachers as above average or outstanding in classroom effectiveness. During their classroom careers, many good-fit stayers assume additional roles as union representatives, curriculum developers, department chairs, and mentors.

Although good-fit stayers entered teaching with a long-term commitment to it, in the sense that they intended from the start to stay in teaching for a long time, if not until retirement, it would be a mistake to conclude that their current career choices and attitudes flow primarily from that strong initial commitment. Analysis of their vignettes suggests otherwise.

The initial enthusiasm and positive attitudes that good-fit teachers bring to teaching are shaped and often challenged by subsequent experiences in the workplace. The stories in this career pattern illustrate what happens to these early career attitudes and highlight teachers' strong professional concerns.

Professional involvement plays a key role for good-fit stayers in shaping career outcomes, in terms of both satisfaction with teaching and the decision to stay or leave. In particular, intrinsic rewards from working with students are the primary draw to remaining in teaching. Comments such as "my main enjoyment is contact with kids" or "I love to watch the excitement of their learning" capture these teachers' positive attitudes about their work. Good-fit teachers, moreover, typically are uninterested in administrative work because they are unwilling to lose touch with the students. These teachers are also more apt to say such things as "I love my students" or "the kids are great" and to view their students as a source of fun, stimulation, and appreciation.

A factor closely related to the intrinsic rewards of work with students is a teacher's sense of success or efficacy (Ashton & Webb, 1986). Good-fit teachers talk about wanting to teach and to make a difference with students. And they come to believe that they are effective in the classroom, that they do make a difference.

The importance of perceived self-efficacy to career outcomes is apparent, particularly when these teachers discuss critical periods during which they felt unsuccessful. For example, Evelyn Brown, a well-regarded English teacher at Rolling Hills, was assigned a heavy load with remedial students when she was still a relatively inexperienced teacher. Consequently, she became so overwhelmed and discouraged by her work that she took steps to change professions.

As with many other teachers, a switch in assignments was the critical change needed to allow Evelyn the opportunity to rebuild her confidence in her ability to be successful with students. The point of

Evelyn's experience is not that remedial assignments in themselves lead to a low sense of classroom success; rather, she had neither the experience nor the skills to deal successfully with that level of educational need. The appropriateness or inappropriateness of an assignment is contingent on the experience or skill of the teacher, which varies over time. Today, bolstered by smaller class sizes and more years of teaching experience, she would not be afraid to accept the same assignment that proved devastating early in her career. Evelyn's story exemplifies how competent teachers can be rendered incompetent through administrative decisions and consequently lose their sense of efficacy and career commitment.

Workplace arrangements figure prominently in good-fit stayers' explanations of career choices and attitudes. Opportunities for professional growth and continued improvement are frequently mentioned sources of satisfaction and efficacy; the survey data show a relationship between the adequacy of opportunities for professional development and sense of success. Being stuck professionally, "doing the same old thing," led Diane Jacobs to search for work outside the classroom after 7 years of teaching. A well-regarded foreign language teacher at Roosevelt, Diane changed her mind about leaving teaching after she was offered the opportunity to implement an innovative teaching method that has increased her ability to work effectively with students and has created new enthusiasm for her work.

Good-fit teachers do not stop learning and acquiring new skills as they gain in seniority. Pointing out that learning to teach well is an evolutionary task, a veteran good-fit stayer asserted, "It takes an enormous amount of time to acquire one's personal teaching skills."

Teachers' ongoing professional development and improvement depend heavily on administrative arrangements and support that entail more than the usual in-service training. According to teachers, important professional growth results from workplace arrangements that also provide financial support to attend professional conferences, time to develop curricula, academic leadership at the department level, and time to work with colleagues. Teachers, especially those with many years of experience, consider collegial support and exchange to be the most valuable of all the sources of professional stimulation (Yee, 1986).

Opportunities to experience different roles and to take part in workplace decision making are other important sources of professional growth and efficacy for good-fit stayers. Teachers in this career pattern frequently assume responsibilities and roles alongside their classroom ones. These additional roles often increase teachers' power and participation in workplace decisions. Diane Jacobs, both a mentor and department chair at Roosevelt, directly linked participation in decision making and professional development opportunities to her sense of success and decision to stay in teaching. The survey data show a correlation between taking on different roles in addition to teaching — specifically, department chair, mentor, curriculum developer, and resource teacher — and a sense of success and decision to stay or leave the profession. (Appendix C provides the relevant statistics.) The growth opportunities Diane described as important to her sense of career consisted of "learning new things, new approaches, meeting with colleagues, and being part of decision making which affects my classroom — decisions about policy and curriculum."

School features, such as the kind of supervision given to beginning teachers, strongly affect teachers' sense of efficacy and growth. Steve Philips at Brown echoed a familiar good-fit story about the first year of teaching. He formed a personal and professional relationship with his supervisor, whom Steve credits with the early development of his skills and self-confidence. For many other good-fit stayers, active support from a supervisor or a close relationship with a mentor was a critical source of feedback, help, and training during a particularly stressful period. These early socialization experiences helped solidify the positive attitudes they brought to teaching.

Personal factors also play a role in the evolution of career choices and attitudes. Certainly, the positive attitudes teachers bring with them to teaching predispose them to a long-term commitment. Other individual characteristics and values influence how organizational or occupational inducements are evaluated, particularly the extrinsic rewards. Life-cycle concerns are evident in the vignettes. For example, when teachers get married and have children, the school schedule assumes greater value because of the time it allows them to spend with their families. For those without young dependents, outside interests such as summer travel make teaching more attractive. Generally, as they get older, job security and retirement benefits become greater inducements to stay.

Although the structure of occupational benefits — vacation, convenient school hours, and job security — holds strong attraction, good-fit stayers regard these extrinsic rewards as distinctly secondary to their intrinsic rewards from work with students. The primary reason for staying, according to these teachers, is the intrinsic rewards from students. The occupational benefits, if mentioned, are generally assigned lesser significance.

Often regarded as a powerful inducement, pay does not figure prominently in career attitudes. Good-fit stayers do not list this extrinsic reward as the primary or even secondary reason for their career choice. Despite a considerable range in pay, these teachers are generally satisfied with their salaries. For example, Patrick Valley at Rolling Hills believes it would be difficult to get another job to match his $40,000 salary. Roosevelt's Brenda Ring, on the other hand, earns $21,600 as a young teacher, but she also believes that the pay is adequate for work she considers intrinsically rewarding. Given the range in salaries, the sense of being adequately compensated indicates the subjective nature of the evaluation of monetary compensation.

A notable exception to the good-fit stayer pattern is Steve Philips. A highly respected Brown faculty member, Steve is similar to other good-fit stayers in initial career attitudes and professional involvement: he takes pride in his work with students, has taken on additional roles in the school, is a leader in the union, and cares about his professional development. However, while other good-fit teachers speak of the presence of enabling conditions in their workplace, these conditions are remarkably absent at Brown by Steve's account. His professional growth is the result of his personal initiative to locate courses and seminars that usually take place outside of school. In fact, Steve's conflicts with the principal make Brown an extremely frustrating place to work. Personal factors — Steve's initiative, his exceptionally strong social commitment and political values — were key in shaping his professional involvement and decision to stay in teaching. Support for his political and social values derives mainly from sources outside the school — his family and friends. His experience exemplifies the possibility, although rare, of developing a strong sense of efficacy and intrinsic reward within a workplace with relatively few enabling conditions.

In general, good-fit stayers' career choices and professional involvement develop from positive workplace experiences that yield sufficient intrinsic rewards.

GOOD-FIT UNDECIDEDS

This group of teachers entered the profession for positive reasons but find themselves with an ambivalent or contingent attitude toward a long-term commitment to teaching. Supervisors generally rate them as above average in classroom effectiveness. Teachers in this career pattern are often, but not always, novice teachers who spend more than 50 hours a week on their jobs, an amount of time similar to that worked by good-fit stayers.

Novice Teachers

The first-year experiences of Roosevelt's Faye Smythe and Brown's Larry Jordan are typical of many other novice teachers who find the workload overwhelming and who question their ability to do well in the classroom. Their ambivalent attitude toward teaching as a long-term career is a common response of new teachers to a stressful first year, even though they may have entered the profession with positive attitudes toward teaching and with intentions to stay for many years. Since most of the attrition occurs within the first few years, this career pattern is particularly important to understand. Unfortunately, this sample includes few novice teachers because fiscal cutbacks and student enrollment declines at the three study schools have resulted in the hiring of relatively few new teachers in recent years.

The reasons good-fit undecideds offer for seriously considering leaving revolve around professional concerns about their sense of achievement as teachers. Although these teachers are rated well by their supervisors, they themselves are dissatisfied with their progress or success.

Workload is a major contributor to this dissatisfaction. They complain of acute stress resulting from the endless nature of the work — the constant pressure to correct papers and produce lesson plans, as well as the difficulty of working with diverse student needs within a group setting.

Although administrators believe that these new teachers have adequate classroom control, good-fit undecideds complain about their discipline problems, about having to nag students to be quiet or to hand in their work. Large classes contribute to the problem, since many students have low skills and are unable to keep up with the rest of the class; consequently, these students often become discipline problems when placed in classes with 30 or more other students — situations in which teachers cannot offer more personal attention. These conditions, coupled with frequent student absences, make it difficult for good-fit undecideds to feel effective or to dismiss thoughts of quitting.

Although workload problems top his list of reasons for leaving the profession, Larry Jordan cited another school factor that diminishes his enthusiasm for teaching. He views the administrative atmosphere at Brown as a significant source of stress and ambivalence. According to him, the administration has created "an environment of intimidation instead of support" and fails to give the constructive feedback he needs as a new teacher.

While internal doubts about the ability to work effectively with students motivate good-fit undecideds to leave teaching, the satisfaction they do receive from working with students is still a countervailing pull to remain in teaching. Faye Smythe's primary reason for wanting to stay in teaching is the work with the students: "I like seeing students learn. . . . I like to watch them grow in ideas." The intrinsic rewards, however, are not sufficiently strong, at least not by themselves, to completely counter the doubts good-fit undecideds harbor about continuing in the profession.

Extrinsic rewards often bolster the moderately strong intrinsic rewards in moving these teachers from a negative to a more neutral or ambivalent position regarding a career in the classroom. For example, occupational benefits such as holidays, vacations, and a work schedule allowing time with family are a strong draw, especially for women who anticipate having children. Faye mentioned that she would be more likely to consider staying longer in teaching if and when she has children.

Nevertheless, these intrinsic and extrinsic inducements are not strong enough to overcome the novice teachers' deep, gnawing dissatisfaction with their sense of failure with students. Relatively weak inducements result in only a tentative or ambivalent commitment to remain in the classroom.

Experienced Teachers

Although good-fit undecideds are generally novice teachers, more experienced teachers can also be part of this career pattern, as 12-year veteran Jackie Paul of Roosevelt illustrates. Jackie differs from her less experienced colleagues in that she is confident about her teaching ability and skills and is enthusiastic about the work. The intrinsic rewards are high for her. Jackie, who is rated as a 9 out of 10 by her supervisor, is also basically satisfied with the workplace conditions at Roosevelt.

Unlike most other teachers, Jackie's ambivalence about staying in teaching hinges on money rather than working conditions. With 10 years of experience behind her, she was hired at Roosevelt at about $5,000 less than a beginning teacher on a regular contract, a situation Jackie finds unjust and inequitable given her skills. Moreover, she finds that her income of less than $15,000 a year for full-time teaching fails to meet the financial needs of her growing family. The pay is inadequate in two senses: in comparison to colleagues at her school and with regard to her family's changing needs. Her dissatisfaction with the extrinsic rewards has led her to consider alternative employment, despite the adequacy of intrinsic rewards.

GOOD-FIT LEAVERS

Most teachers in this career pattern at one time had wanted to make teaching a lifelong or long-term career. They gave positive reasons for entering teaching similar to those of the good-fit stayers, but they have quit or are preparing to leave within the next 5 years. (These leavers do not include teachers who plan to retire.) Teachers in this career pattern illustrate how initial attitudes are transformed as a result of experience in the workplace.

Good-fit leavers are not uniformly the best or the worst teachers according to supervisor ratings: They include above-average, average, and below-average teachers in terms of classroom effectiveness. What the good-fit leavers do have in common, however, is their personal dissatisfaction with their achievements with students. The vignettes illustrate how the meaning of competence is internally defined by teachers and is not necessarily congruent with external, supervisor evaluations; the case stories also indicate the great importance that teachers place on classroom success and their sense of efficacy. A former teacher highly rated by her supervisor explained that she left the profession because after "giving it [her] all" she still was unable to accomplish what she had hoped for with her students.

Similarly, a low-rated teacher who is preparing to quit complained that he was not "getting back enough" from his students and began doubting his ability to achieve the results he wanted.

The sources of these teachers' dissatisfaction with their achievements in the classroom are rooted primarily in workplace factors. District and state policies in recent years have directly affected teachers' classroom conditions and consequently performance. A Roosevelt home economics teacher complained that California's new emphasis on academics resulted in a decline in status of her subject area and the subsequent decrease in her career commitment.

State-level reductions in fiscal resources have hit the elective fields the hardest, requiring teachers to teach outside their major subject areas or to work under less than ideal conditions—a frustrating situation producing discouragement and burnout for many good-fit teachers committed to quality instruction.

Inappropriate teaching assignments in general are a significant factor pushing good-fit teachers out of the classroom. Teachers who are otherwise competent become incompetent when given courses for which they are unprepared. The assignment of the chemistry teacher to teach an advanced course out of his field is a case of administratively induced incompetence. After 2 years of this assignment and much anxiety over doing the students an injustice — and 18 years as a teacher — he quit.

Inadequate administrative and collegial support created a feeling of isolation, a chronic problem particularly for good-fit leavers who received low performance ratings. Some of these teachers received little assistance from supervisors or colleagues during their difficult induction years and never gained the necessary skills for or self-confidence from success with students. Teachers like David Jensen at Brown adapted to their lack of success by lowering their expectations for students or by seeking positions that removed them from the classroom (such as counseling and administration).

Other low-performing teachers found themselves increasingly alienated from their clients, frustrated by students' behavior. Moreover, an acute sense of professional and social isolation often accompanied this alienation from students. Throughout his 16 years in the classroom, Roosevelt's Rob Bole was unable to recall anything in his school setting that helped him become a more effective teacher.

Teachers expressed their desire for more pay as a reason to leave teaching in the context of insufficient intrinsic reward from the classroom. When intrinsic rewards are weak, individuals turn to extrinsic rewards to bring the inducements and contributions into balance. Rob Bole, for instance, stated that his salary was "poor" because it did not adequately compensate for his hard work given the lack of student response. Although some of the good-fit leavers listed inadequate pay as one of several reasons to leave, many others in this career pattern did not mention it at all. In fact, several good-fit leavers close to retirement considered pay and retirement benefits as major reasons to endure teaching for a few more years.

Primary among teachers' reasons to leave was their dissatisfaction with their success in the classroom and the workplace conditions that constrained their ability to be effective. Good-fit leavers, whether they are evaluated by supervisors as effective or ineffective, share a common perspective that they were deprived the satisfaction of successful work with students and that the intrinsic rewards of teaching constituted an insufficiently strong inducement to stay and contribute their effort and talents.

WEAK-FIT STAYERS

Weak-fit stayers recall their entry into teaching as accidental: they fell into it or simply had nothing better to do. Many weak-fit teachers also started with a tentative commitment to teaching, intending to stay only a short while. Early in their careers, they searched for other jobs to switch to. Weak-fit teachers' lack of initial enthusiasm and tentative attitudes toward teaching contrast sharply to the initial career attitudes of their good-fit colleagues.

These weak-fit stayers are in their thirties or forties and have come to believe that few job alternatives have benefits comparable to teaching. They have evolved into stayers, anticipating that they will remain with classroom work until retirement. However, teachers in this career pattern diverge from each other in a significant way: some of the weak-fit stayers are highly rated and involved in their work; others in this career pattern receive just average ratings and like the work because it is easy or convenient.

High-Involvement Teachers

How did the weak-fit stayers develop into high-involvement or low-involvement teachers? Workplace conditions play a critical role in transforming weak-fit teachers with tentative commitments to teaching into committed teachers who enjoy their work. A highly rated special education teacher at Rolling Hills explored other job options for many years. Like other teachers who want to leave teaching, Betty Davidson experienced a gnawing insecurity about her success as a beginning teacher. Only after she was transferred from an itinerant position to a regular classroom job did she become confident about her teaching abilities and subsequently decide to stay in teaching. An appropriate assignment permitting her to experience classroom success made a dramatic difference in her career attitudes and plans.

Administrative and collegial assistance reinforce positive career attitudes of involved weak-fit stayers. Susan Dodd, now an excellent English teacher at Brown, related how her first- and second-year experiences differed dramatically in terms of a support system and her subsequent feelings about teaching. Her first-year principal often screamed at her, and fellow teachers were reluctant to share or help; she came to hate teaching and believed she would never make it a career. But she resolved to stick it out one more year so she that would not leave teaching as a failure. During her second year, through the help and understanding of a new principal, she became self-confident in her abilities and reversed her attitude about teaching. By her third year, a supportive environment in a new school where everyone worked together enabled her finally to learn to "truly love teaching" despite the intense needs of the students.

Susan's induction experience emphasizes the importance of conditions that support socialization during the induction period. The absence of administrative and collegial support in her second year would have pushed her out of teaching. The presence of a supportive work environment allowed her to grow in competence as well as in commitment to teaching. Her initially weak enthusiasm for teaching evolved into strong professional involvement and a decision to stay in the profession.

Today, the stimulation and personal support Susan receives from her department chair at Brown continue to nurture her enthusiasm for teaching, as does a close professional and social relationship with a dedicated and enthusiastic colleague in her department. Like many other high-involvement teachers, Susan rates collegial exchange and support as the greatest source of her professional stimulation and a major reason to stay.

While organizational arrangements can facilitate collegial interaction, individuals also construct their social environment by selecting certain types of close friends and social exchanges. Efficacious, satisfied teachers tend to associate with teachers like themselves. The survey data reveal that teachers who feel successful in their work are more likely to feel satisfied with their job as well as to report that their close colleagues are also satisfied with teaching. Conversely, those who feel less efficacious are more likely to be dissatisfied with teaching and to perceive that their close colleagues are also dissatisfied. With some teachers, association with other involved teachers is a conscious strategy to create a positive, supportive working environment for themselves.

Occupational benefits are significant reasons to stay, especially as teachers approach middle age. Comparable jobs appear less possible and attractive in comparison to the pay, vacations, security, and health and retirement benefits in teaching. As important as these occupational benefits are to involved weak-fit stayers, these extrinsic rewards rank below the intrinsic inducements received from students. The enjoyment of personal contact with students and the belief that they can make a difference in the classroom form the basis for decisions to remain in teaching.

Low-Involvement Teachers

In sharp contrast to the high-involvement teachers are weak-fit stayers whose performance ratings are only average and who spend as little time as possible on the job. The interaction between personal and occupational factors plays a main role in determining these career attitudes. While inducements for high-involvement teachers derive from intrinsic rewards, these low-involvement teachers are primarily drawn to teaching because of extrinsic rewards: the job security, the pay, and the convenience of the hours and of vacations to outside interests.

An 18-year veteran in the classroom explained that her central life interests revolve around her children. She added that she lacks the financial independence to experiment with other jobs, although she would like to. Her primary reasons for staying in teaching center around a combination of factors external to work with students: an adequate salary, health benefits, job security, vacations, and a schedule compatible with child-rearing duties.

A remedial reading teacher at Brown seconds these points. Although he has no children, vacations allow him precious time to pursue outside interests. The security in teaching is also a strong draw: no one can fire him. Finally, revealing that his disinclination to leave or seek job alternatives can also be attributed to his accepting personality, he said: "I'm not the kind of person to get out."

An easy workload holds considerable attraction for this second type of weak-fit stayer. The remedial reading teacher at Brown, rated below average by an administrator, has settled into a comfortable routine. He admitted to being "basically a lazy person" who is "not dedicated" to his job. Another Brown faculty member likes teaching labs because so little preparation is involved and he can work less than 40 hours a week.

Many teachers at Brown consider their jobs difficult — not at all easy. What accounts for the different evaluations of teaching within the same school? Part of the explanation lies in the personalities or personal circumstances of teachers, for example, whether they have strong outside interests or passive personalities. Such individual characteristics lead teachers to seek relatively easy assignments or to adapt their teaching methods so that little effort is required. Teachers who spoke of easy workloads often had assignments (for instance, remedial reading or general math) that necessitated little preparation and often utilized programmed materials. While other teachers complained about the boredom and routine of undemanding assignments, weak-fit stayers with low involvement preferred repetitious assignments necessitating little preparation.

The perception of an absence of job alternatives comparable in salary to teaching is an important, but often unspoken, source of attachment to teaching. A 40-year-old teacher who earns nearly $40,000 a year revealed how age interacts with this perception and contributes to a strong commitment to stay, so strong that it would "take an earthquake" to push him to leave.

Intrinsic rewards from work with students and success in the classroom are sparse for this subgroup of weak-fit stayers and are not mentioned as one of the three top reasons for staying. Rather, these teachers frequently cite students' lack of interest or motivation as the main reason students fail to learn. This view of students as a hindrance to teachers' effectiveness is in direct contrast to that of good-fit stayers, who tend to see students as a valued source of reward.

In sum, weak-fit stayers share common initial career attitudes and have made the same career choice to remain in the profession. However, the quality of their careers in terms of professional involvement diverges dramatically. The high-involvement group has come to love teaching. The low-involvement group unenthusiastically puts up with the job. Whereas intrinsic rewards are primary inducements to the former group, extrinsic rewards hold the low-involvement group in teaching.

WEAK-FIT LEAVERS

Teachers in this career pattern have already left teaching or are actively preparing to leave. (These leavers do not include teachers who plan to retire.) They entered the profession in the same manner as weak-fit stayers, accidentally or by default. Upon entry, they did not exhibit the strong draw to teaching that the good-fit stayers did. These particular weak-fit leavers started with a tentative commitment to teaching but ended up staying more than 10 years before finally leaving. Prior to quitting, these teachers usually paved the way for their exit by taking courses or gaining experience in a second job; they also spent fewer hours than average on their teaching.

Supervisors' ratings of weak-fit leavers range from below average to excellent, a similar distribution to that of leavers in the good-fit pattern. Despite the variation in supervisors' ratings, the weak-fit leavers, like other leavers, share a dissatisfaction with their sense of success. A former English teacher, remembered as an excellent teacher by a Brown administrator, taught for 10 years but recalled that he "never really loved teaching," experiencing "a lack of fulfillment at the end of each day." Another ex-teacher from Brown, who in an administrator's estimation "did not have his heart in teaching," recounted similarly that after 20 years in teaching he lacked a "sense of accomplishment."

An accumulation of experiences in the workplace led weak-fit leavers to finally quit. Their early years in teaching were often traumatic, sink-or-swim situations in which they received little help from supervisors or colleagues. One teacher characterized the initiation he received in an inner-city school as "jungle warfare." Left to his own devices, he learned to establish authority by hitting students. Another teacher's first year, during which he lacked proper materials and support, imprinted him with a sense of futility that never left in later years. These teachers were unable to reverse the negative socialization experiences of their early classroom careers.

An additional concern for the younger teachers is the instability of the job due to the threat of layoffs. A young Roosevelt teacher left teaching after only 2 years because the difficulties of the early years coupled with job insecurity proved to be too much.

Some weak-fit leavers had a more auspicious start in teaching but still decided to leave. A former home economics/social studies teacher at Rolling Hills found her early years very rewarding. The turning point in her attitude toward classroom work occurred when she was assigned to teach in her minor field. Evaluated by an administrator as a good teacher in her major subject area, but as "having trouble" in her minor, this teacher never felt confident in her minor, which eventually comprised three of her five course assignments. She sought unsuccessfully to be relieved of those assignments and attributed her failure to administrative "regimen" and "hassles" that treated teachers more "like numbers than humans."

The sparsity of professional stimulation also plays a large role in decisions to leave. Marilyn Moore, an English teacher at Brown, cited the absence of opportunities for professional improvement as the reason for the "dead-end quality" to teaching. Marilyn, who is preparing herself for community college teaching, noted that the sparsity of growth opportunities explains why teachers like herself turn away from teaching for their stimulation and reward and eventually resign.

School factors strongly influence a teacher's sense of efficacy and career attitudes in additional ways. Teachers mentioned workplace conditions, including inadequate time for preparation, inappropriate classroom materials, and large class sizes that severely constrain their ability to be effective with students.

Leavers often identified students as an impediment to a teacher's effectiveness. For example, a former Brown teacher described how poor student attendance created a sense of professional impotence:

> There was the futility of getting class together. Sometimes there'd be 50% attendance. The same group of kids there one day wouldn't be there the next. It was impossible to build from one lesson to the next. Few attended class every day.

Moreover, the students who do attend class often fail to complete their assignments, thus compounding the sense of frustration. To this leaver, the home environment, rather than the teacher or school, determined student achievement and behavior.

Another Brown teacher complained that students are so emotionally needy and wild that she has to spend all her time on discipline. She noted that the multiethnic, multicultural composition of the student body contributes to discipline problems and misunderstandings between students and teachers.

The sparse returns from work with students produce an overwhelming feeling of being "uncompensated for the extraordinarily difficult work." Money accounts for only a portion of what compensation means to teachers. In one leaver's opinion, his feeling of being inadequately rewarded was due to the lack of appreciation and recognition in a broader sense — being taken for granted — rather than salary considerations.

The low social status of teachers, which some teachers said made their friends "wonder why you're still in teaching," compounds the feeling of being poorly compensated. A former Brown teacher linked the issue of pay to that of professional and societal recognition: "I didn't feel like a professional, getting acknowledgment by society that teachers are important. They deserve to be paid as experts just as doctors are." The desire for more pay, while a factor in weak-fit leavers' decisions to quit, is never the primary reason. Monetary compensation is viewed as inadequate only when the intrinsic rewards are unsatisfactory as well.

SCHOOLS AS PLACES FOR CAREERS

Schools are not equally easy or rewarding places in which to work; likewise, teaching careers are not equally satisfying. Workplace differences overshadow the ostensible similarity of teaching positions. School arrangements can create conditions conducive to successful teaching and therefore act as inducements for teachers to stay and contribute their energy and talents; alternatively, they can present obstacles to classroom success and undermine commitment to teaching.

Teachers want to teach. And they want to make a difference with students. This desire is evident again and again in the individual vignettes. Most are good-fit teachers who come to the profession out of a desire to work with young people or to be of service. Some of these teachers find school conditions that are supportive of their goals and values; others find institutional hindrances. The difference often determines whether they also find satisfying careers.

Intrinsic rewards, arising out of teachers' sense of efficacy, are powerful inducements for teachers to stay in the classroom and to deepen their professional involvement. These psychic rewards appear more compelling than extrinsic rewards, such as pay. Teachers who feel confident that they are making a difference in the classroom cite their work with students as a major source of reward and the primary reason they are staying in teaching. Moreover, teachers for whom intrinsic rewards from classroom work are plentiful are usually motivated to seek professional growth and to spend more time and effort in the classroom— behavior that reinforces or further stimulates self-efficacy.

Conversely, teachers who doubt their achievements in the classroom do not experience their work with students as a major inducement to stay or to contribute their best efforts. These teachers emphasize extrinsic sources of reward as their reasons to stay; they are also more likely to withhold personal contributions by leaving, or, worse, by settling into on-the-job retirement.

These career attitudes and decisions are not the result of yes-or-no choices at a single point in time. Career outcomes fluctuate with shifting conditions of work—including workplace and job changes—and with changes in individual circumstances and values.

Teaching careers—including professional involvement and decisions to remain in or to leave teaching—are the result of a process of development, influenced by the interaction among multiple factors that change over time: workplace, occupational, professional, and personal. All these factors, however, are conditioned fundamentally and continually by a teacher's particular workplace and job conditions.

CHAPTER 6

Conclusions and Implications

These school portraits and individual vignettes illustrate the multi-dimensional nature of the problem of retention that traditional conceptualizations of teacher turnover and careers fail to capture. Most research on organizational turnover and retention of teachers assumes a uniform performance level among employees and frequently relies on closed-ended survey responses that group teachers simply as stayers or leavers — gross categories that mask important nuances. Apart from age or years in the classroom, personal variables are rarely analyzed as influences or conditioning effects. By contrast, this book highlights the multiple and individual meanings of career choice. The vignettes direct attention to the variation in career outcomes, particularly in professional involvement — the level of teachers' engagement and commitment to perform well. This view of career outcomes reveals, for example, enthusiastic, highly effective stayers who cannot imagine anything they would rather do than teach, as well as reluctant stayers who are frustrated with their lack of classroom success and relieved to see their students leave at the end of the day.

When organizational behavior researchers consider turnover, they focus on such inducements as pay, job security, and promotion opportunities. These extrinsic sources of reward, however, appear salient primarily when teachers fail to achieve the personal satisfaction of doing a job well. The intrinsic factors that such analyses overlook are, in fact, heavily weighted by teachers, many of whom leave the profession when rewards in the classroom are low.

Conventional approaches to occupational attrition or retention also tend to regard career decisions as a static event. By looking at factors at one period in time and relying heavily on sources of immediate dissatisfaction and attraction, they miss the dynamics and evolution of career outcomes.

Finally, studies of attrition among teachers differ from the vignettes presented here in that they fail to capture individual viewpoints and to integrate into their analyses the interaction of individual factors (such as family circumstances, outside interests, values, age, life-cycle stages) with workplace and occupational factors.

A PERSPECTIVE ON CAREERS FOR TEACHERS

The portraits and vignettes here offer an alternative view of why teachers stay and leave the profession and call for an interactive and dynamic conceptualization of career processes in the teaching profession. This alternative perspective considers the influence that the school environment, workplace conditions, occupational benefits, and personal characteristics have over time on professional involvement and the decision to stay or leave.

Workplace Context: Environmental Influences on Schools

Teachers' career attitudes are, in part, adaptations over time to work experiences. A complex configuration of school factors shape initial career attitudes, the gradual development of professional involvement, and the ultimate decision to remain in or leave teaching. However, workplace influences affecting teachers' personal contributions do not emanate solely from within the school.

Schools are open to their environments. Community, district, and state conditions influence school conditions. Exclusion of these contextual factors weakens the ability of the standard models of retention to explain variation in career outcomes. For example, the school portraits show that teachers' perceptions of workload, efficacy, and satisfaction are shaped by student characteristics (the level, diversity, and intensity of their educational need) as well as by parent behavior. These factors, generally unrecognized in studies of teachers' attrition, are strong community influences on teachers' working conditions and opportunities for intrinsic reward (see also Hallinger & Murphy, 1986; Metz, 1988).

District and state policies also shape teachers' classroom experiences and career attitudes. Policies at these higher levels affect the provision of adequate resources and staffing to carry out school programs — conditions essential to successful teaching. Policy changes at the state level, in academic requirements for example, can affect teachers' course assignments, capacities, and career attitudes, even at sites, such as Rolling Hills, with very supportive school conditions. This example illustrates the vulnerability of the workplace and careers to policy decisions aimed at improving educational outcomes.

Workplace Conditions: Support and Obstacles

Although contextual factors may strongly influence career outcomes, organizational choices that are made within the schools directly affect teachers' work experiences as well. Administrative policies and practices play a key role in career outcomes and attitudes, particularly as they relate to the development of competence and sense of efficacy, for example, buffering classroom learning from outside interruptions and providing support for discipline contribute to job satisfaction by enabling teachers to be effective. Teachers regard the absence of this kind of basic support as a major source of dissatisfaction and as a tremendous obstacle to their effectiveness. These kinds of organizational conditions are frequently mentioned in interviews with teachers but are typically excluded from traditional research on turnover.

Course assignments powerfully affect a teacher's sense of workload, job satisfaction, and intrinsic reward. Placing teachers in courses for which they are unprepared or lacking in expertise quickly erodes self-confidence and self-efficacy, particularly if proper training, support, and encouragement are not provided.

The interviews with teachers provide examples of how induction arrangements exert a strong influence on the development of professional bonding and involvement (see also Becker & Carper, 1966; Berlew & Hall, 1977; Hall & Schneider, 1973; Wanous, 1980). The nature of novice teachers' assignments, coupled with the level of support given during the induction period, affects the speed with which professional competence and self-confidence are achieved. Teachers with positive novice experiences — reasonable assignments in terms of load and subject matter, adequate feedback, and, especially, personal support from mentors and colleagues — are more likely to develop the competence and skills required for a satisfying career; teachers with more negative early experiences (frequently those whose induction occurred in an inner-city school) are less likely to acquire the tools of the trade or to develop professional involvement and a commitment to staying in teaching. The vignettes capture how the sink-or-swim model of induction can produce teachers who are among the least professionally committed.

Even more experienced teachers are not immune from the effects of poor assignments, although the consequences are generally not as dramatic for veterans as they are for beginning teachers. Course assignments outside a teacher's subject specialty hold such significance that they prompt teachers, even in otherwise ideal working conditions, to defect. A heavy load of remedial or general courses, where the returns in terms of student achievement are slow or sparse (a situation more common in inner-city schools), often results in demoralization. Large class size, in the context of diverse and intense educational needs of students, is another major element affecting teachers' sense of workload and therefore their ability to experience high levels of success with students. Administrative decisions and practices affecting workload, class size, assignments, and support can shift the balance of organizational inducements and teachers' contributions, prompting reduced effort and professional commitment.

Organizational support for professional development also exerts a considerable influence over whether teachers regard their work positively or negatively. Most teachers, particularly high-involvement teachers, want and seek professional stimulation. Supportive administrative arrangements (those that create opportunities for learning, allot time for workshops and collegial exchange of ideas, and supply financial support to attend conferences or in-services) enable teachers—even those with many years of experience—to learn and improve.

Although high-involvement teachers more actively seek professional growth opportunities, even low-involvement teachers who are attracted by easy workloads admit some interest in improvement and feedback. This indicates that low involvement is not a static state and contains the potential to be transformed with proper administrative encouragement and support.

Opportunities for collegial interaction are teachers' most valued form of professional stimulation. High-involvement teachers generally report more exchange with colleagues than do low-involvement ones, who often experience isolation from their peers and are more likely to be dissatisfied with teaching. Most teachers, however, report that their opportunities for peer exchange are inadequate. Faculties are often fragmented in the sense that they seldom are able to observe each other teach, to give feedback, to plan lessons, or to solve problems together. The vignettes, however, show that when social and professional interaction among peers does occur, this kind of interaction is a critical source of professional identification and growth (see also Becker & Carper, 1966; Nias, 1985).

For many teachers, especially the high-involvement ones, professional development carries additional meaning: taking part in decision making, exerting some influence over the teaching environment, and assuming additional roles (Yee, 1986). Rarely, however, do teachers want to move into administration. The majority of good-fit stayers experience a variety of roles during their career, such as department chair, mentor teacher, curriculum developer, and union activist. These additional roles allow teachers to assume a measure of leadership without precluding the central role of teachers, that is, teaching. Teachers who receive adequate intrinsic rewards from their work in the classroom typically are uninterested in promotion out of teaching.

High-involvement teachers, many of whom are good-fit stayers, are frequently concerned with having a voice in decisions affecting class-room conditions; these teachers believe that they hold a personal and professional stake in matters that affect the quality of teaching and learning. Frustrated by policies handed down by administrators and policy makers who are divorced from the day-to-day realities of the classroom, these teachers want a more collaborative or collegial approach to decision making in the schools. They want to exercise some control over what matters the most to them — student learning.

Workplaces, such as Rolling Hills, that empower teachers to take part in decisions affecting their work conditions contribute to professional bonding, stimulation, and satisfaction — a theme also reflected in the broader organizational literature (Kanter, 1983; Newman et al., 1985; Shedd, 1987). In contrast, workplaces such as Brown, where bureaucratic control is the order of the day and staff have little input, foster dissatisfaction, stress, and low involvement (see also Argyris, 1957; Bacharach, Bauer, & Conley, 1986; Cox and Wood, 1980; Karasek, 1979; McNeil, 1986).

In general, such school factors as appropriate workload or opportunities for input operate indirectly in the inducement-contribution balance by enabling teachers to do a good job, and thus increasing highly valued intrinsic rewards. Other school factors, such as collegial interaction and professional stimulation, figure both indirectly and directly as inducements, since teachers value these workplace features as rewards in themselves, not merely for their instrumental value in reaching students.

The configuration of workplace conditions that are important to teachers highlights their primary orientation toward students and their professional concerns with being able to do their job well. School conditions that teachers consider to be supportive of good teaching serve as inducements to sustain their career and contribute their best efforts to the job.

While the workplace conditions discussed are important in all settings, the salience of particular features varies across schools. Reasons for satisfaction and dissatisfaction depend on relative strengths and weaknesses of the workplace and upon context conditions. For example, a primary concern at Brown is class size, whereas at Roosevelt major faculty concerns revolve around support for discipline.

Some workplace features matter more or less at different times in a teacher's career or life. Other features appear to be relatively constant in importance: For instance, support for student discipline and a reasonable workload are of considerable concern to both beginning and veteran teachers. On the other hand, formal sources of professional development appear to be more critical to novice than veteran teachers, who more highly value other sources of professional growth and challenge (collegial exchange, opportunities to take on additional roles and to participate in decisions).

Occupational Benefits and Personal Factors

Personal factors may influence how occupational benefits are assessed, particularly how vacations, schedule, job security, and health and retirement benefits weigh as inducements. The vignettes suggest that the salience of these occupational benefits, or extrinsic rewards, varies with a teacher's age, parenting status, and outside interests. Rewards may acquire different meaning or value at different points in a teacher's life cycle. Job satisfaction reflects varying degrees of fit between occupational benefits and changing individual needs or roles (Ball & Goodson, 1985; Sikes, 1985).

Workplace conditions also influence the importance teachers place on occupational benefits. Positive experiences and enabling conditions in the schools generate intrinsic rewards and perceived efficacy among teachers. When sense of success is high, the inducement from occupational benefits is considered complementary to, but less important than, the intrinsic rewards. Conversely, when intrinsic rewards and sense of efficacy are weak as a result of unsupportive workplace conditions, occupational benefits assume a major role in teachers' decisions to stay in teaching. Professional involvement appears to be lowered under this condition. When intrinsic rewards and self-efficacy are judged to be sufficiently weak, occupational benefits appear less attractive and teachers simply leave.

Popular opinion holds that teachers defect primarily because of inadequate pay. However, although pay may be mentioned as one of several reasons to stay, this extrinsic reward is generally not the major concern for leavers. The desire for more pay is usually expressed in the context of insufficient rewards from work with students or lack of recognition or appreciation in a broader sense. In other words, for leavers as well as for stayers, pay acquires salience in the absence of intrinsic forms of compensation. Studies on human services employees — for example, nurses, social workers, priests, and police — support the conclusion that those primarily oriented toward client service, including teachers, consider intrinsic rewards more important than monetary compensation; only when the work ceases to be intrinsically satisfying (or when the salary is sufficiently low) does money become a major issue (Edelwich, 1980; Hall & Schneider, 1973).

Occasionally, however, salary takes on major significance even in the presence of plentiful intrinsic rewards from work with students. One teacher in the study who earns less than $15,000 a year is an example of this. A 10-year veteran in teaching, this teacher transferred to Roosevelt because of her husband's job relocation. However, she is paid at the rate of a temporary, beginning teacher. She feels unfairly compensated compared to colleagues with the same experience. The discrepancy or inequity in salary is large enough to push her to consider jobs other than teaching. Her experience appears uncommon but suggests that policies that punish mobility between districts may be costly in terms of retaining good teachers.

While concerns with salary appear to be at least a consideration in decisions to stay or leave — especially as teachers have children and approach middle age — they are notably absent as teachers talk about what motivates them to perform their best. Although satisfactory and equitable pay may be a necessary condition of career commitment, it is insufficient to motivate high levels of job engagement (see also Deci, 1976). Rather, teachers speak of work conditions that stimulate and enable them to teach competently — such as reasonable workloads, administrative support and feedback, opportunities for professional development, collegial interaction, and participation in decision making. These workplace features act as powerful inducements to contribute effort and talents in the classroom because teachers directly link these elements to their ability to be effective and consequently their level of intrinsic reward and satisfaction. By contrast, monetary incentives and other occupational benefits are in teachers' views unassociated with support to do better and thus are not considered motivators for classroom performance.

Professional Involvement and Intrinsic Rewards

Within the complex interactions among workplace, occupational, and personal factors, the dynamic between professional involvement and career choice emerges as a major theme. Patterns of involvement and choice vary among individuals as well as across workplaces. Teachers can be grouped roughly as those with high and those with low professional involvement. The high-involvement group is distinguished from the low group in several ways:

- A personal perception of efficacy or success as a teacher versus a perception of limited efficacy or success
- A view of students as the major source of intrinsic reward versus a view of students as a major impediment to teacher effectiveness
- Above-average versus below-average time and effort spent on the job
- A sense of professional growth versus a sense of routine, boredom, and lack of professional stimulation

Performance ratings by supervisors, often used as an "objective" measure of teaching quality, are moderately related to teachers' subjective assessments of their efficacy. Highly rated teachers may still feel inadequate or insufficiently successful in the classroom. A teacher's sense of efficacy, rather than external performance ratings, serves as an important gauge of the sufficiency of intrinsic rewards from work with students. Teachers who feel confident that they are making a difference in the classroom, such as most of the good-fit stayers, cite their work with students as the primary reason for continuing in the profession. This observation is consistent with a major theme in the literature on teachers—the primacy of intrinsic rewards (Johnson, 1986; Lortie, 1975; McLaughlin et al., 1986) and the relationship of sense of efficacy to those rewards (Ashton & Webb, 1986; McLaughlin & Marsh, 1978).

Conversely, teachers who doubt their achievements in the classroom, such as many weak-fit leavers, do not consider their work with students as a major source of reward; instead they tend to see students as the source of their problems and to believe that student performance is influenced by factors beyond their control, usually the home environment or the students themselves. Teachers for whom intrinsic rewards from work with students are plentiful appear motivated to seek professional growth and stimulation and to spend much time and effort in the classroom—behavior that reinforces or increases the sense of efficacy. Teachers for whom intrinsic rewards from students are sparse, however, are more likely to work fewer hours, to be passive about professional growth, and to view teaching as boring or routine—characteristics that reinforce a limited sense of efficacy.

Most high-involvement teachers interviewed were satisfied with their work with students and plan on staying in teaching, whereas low-involvement teachers were more likely to resign from the job or, worse, to exert a minimum of effort and blame students for failure. Some teachers, such as the good-fit undecideds, were neither high nor low in involvement, but a combination, spending an above-average amount of time and energy on the job and receiving some rewards from students, but harboring serious doubts about their efficacy and their commitment to stay or to maintain their level of personal contributions. Their stories again underscore the critical role that perceived efficacy plays in inducing or motivating teachers to stay and contribute their talents and energy. Their experiences also illustrate how novice teachers view their professional involvement and career decisions as tentative and changeable.

Teachers' professional involvement, however, is not mainly the consequence of individual personality or ability; it is shaped by experiences in the workplace. This conclusion stands in contrast to those reached in other studies of teacher retention, which either avoid the issue of professional involvement or emphasize the relationship of academic ability to retention, ignoring or minimizing the influence of variable workplace conditions (see, for example, Berry, 1985; Heyns, 1988; Schlechty & Vance, 1981).

Career outcomes are dynamic for new teachers and experienced teachers alike. Professional involvement and career commitment are not static qualities; they evolve over time, but not necessarily in a consistent direction. Dramatic reversals are possible. The level and direction of effort and performance are the product of experiences in the workplace, not simply the outcome of individual predisposition or personality. The balance between workplace inducements and individual contributions is a fragile construction easily upset. The vignettes, such as that of good-fit leaver Valerie Green from Rolling Hills, show how high involvement and commitment can be undermined and destroyed. The stories of some weak-fit stayers, such as Brown's Susan Dodd and Rolling Hills' Betty Davidson, reveal how low commitment to staying can be reversed.

Job Satisfaction: What Are Teachers Satisfied With?

Job satisfaction ratings on surveys typically reveal that teachers are generally satisfied with their jobs. What does this mean in light of the variation in career outcomes revealed here? How is it, for example, that low-involvement teachers who report few intrinsic rewards from students can characterize themselves as "satisfied" with teaching? More to the point, what are teachers satisfied with? Teachers differentially weigh inducements and can be satisfied with alternative combinations of job rewards. The key factor in how teachers weigh the array of work inducements appears to be the success they experience in teaching students.

Conversely, when perceived efficacy is low, satisfaction with teaching then derives predominantly from extrinsic rewards or from the fit of teaching to interests outside of the classroom, such as hobbies or family life. For these teachers, workplace conditions appear to inhibit teaching success. This study suggests that sources of satisfaction have implications for performance: salience of intrinsic rewards is associated with high professional involvement and contributions; alternatively, salience of extrinsic rewards accompanies minimal levels of professional engagement.

Hallmarks of a Career: Sense of Success and Failure

The importance of intrinsic rewards and efficacy underscores the psychological and subjective nature of teaching careers; on a more theoretical level, this phenomenon illustrates how careers impart meaning to individuals' lives (Hall & Schneider, 1973; Hughes, 1937). Teachers, like other social service professionals, strive for a sense of efficacy or psychological success in their work. In this way, teachers gain self-esteem, a feeling that they have performed competently in a worthwhile endeavor. A satisfying career, then, is one in which individuals seek and experience a sense of achievement and accomplishment during the course of their work. Career development denotes internal growth or increasing levels of expertise rather than promotion up an organizational ladder (McLaughlin & Yee, 1988). Thus the hallmarks of a satisfying career are high professional involvement and sense of success.

Teachers who perceive themselves as failures in the classroom may find the teaching occupation satisfying because of its fit with outside interests or obligations, but for them teaching is a job, not a career. They look to activities outside the workplace for their self-esteem or personal identity, because teaching does not impart the same personal meaning or satisfaction for these teachers as it does for their high-involvement colleagues. Outside interests, in turn, increase the extrinsic rewards of teaching by placing a premium on free time and vacations. A weak sense of efficacy obviates the chance of a real career in terms of being able to experience a positive self-image through one's work.

The individual career stories reveal that a sense of failure is often associated with feelings of hopelessness, lack of control, and emotional depletion — symptoms of burnout that reflect an imbalance between inducements and contributions (see also Edelwich, 1980). Teachers who speak of being "burned out" feel that their meager accomplishments are not worth their efforts and often are looking for a way out of teaching. Stress is usually cited as the cause of burnout, but the vignettes show that stress does not necessarily end in negative career outcomes. Good-fit stayers also report high levels of stress due to time demands, but they avoid burnout because they experience a sense of personal control and professional efficacy. Psychological success is therefore an important mediating mechanism between stress and burnout.

The consequences of a sense of failure go beyond the individual. Teachers who lack a sense of success in their work adapt to their failure in ways that also carry grave implications for organizational effectiveness. Teachers deal with their frustration and disappointment with lack of classroom success by any of the following strategies:

> Quitting the profession
> Lowering expectations or goals for student performance
> Reducing efforts at or interest in improvement
> Blaming students or relinquishing personal responsibility for student performance
> Placing increased value on extrinsic rewards, such as pay

Many of these teachers do not physically leave the profession. Instead, they withdraw emotionally and psychologically, effectively retiring on the job.

Construction of Meaning

Early career attitudes are frequently changed by experiences in the workplace. Some teachers who enter with the intention of staying in teaching end up leaving, while others who join the profession holding more tentative commitments stay. For other teachers, career decisions are tentative or still in the process of formation. Workplace factors, especially early induction practices, play a pivotal role in the reinforcement or amendment of initial career attitudes and the development of competence and feelings of self-efficacy.

While workplace conditions and context exert a powerful influence on teachers and their career outcomes, teachers are also able to shape what is meaningful and real to them within the constraints of the workplace. Teachers' adjustments to psychological failure furnish further evidence of individual manipulations of experiences in the workplace. Teachers also appear to select as friends colleagues who support their adaptations. Moreover, within the same workplace, even within the same department, teachers have different experiences and come to different conclusions about their work. How does this happen?

How, for example, are individuals at an inner-city school able to sustain high involvement and career satisfaction in the face of difficult work conditions, considerable peer dissatisfaction, and low involvement on the part of many colleagues? Some teachers, such as Brown's Steve

Philips, bring to teaching exceptionally strong political and service values that are nourished and reinforced by social ties outside of school and by participation in the union. Other teachers at Brown, such as Susan Dodd, sustain their commitment by forming close personal ties with other committed colleagues or by seeking out positions with reduced teaching loads. These teachers are able to counter the difficult conditions of work in the inner city in ways that many teachers are not.

Individuals themselves change over time, and their changing personal perspectives, values, and attitudes shape the ways in which workplace conditions are evaluated. A career, therefore, is constructed through continuous processes of personal negotiation and interpretation within a work setting.

POLICY IMPLICATIONS

What policies would support teachers' negotiation of satisfying classroom careers? This question has significant implications not only for teachers but also for schools. The issue is not simply or primarily one of employee satisfaction. Implicit in the notion of having a career is professional involvement, growth, and accomplishment. Consequently, it matters greatly to teachers, students, and schools if teachers are able to negotiate a positive sense of career.

The enormous variability in career outcomes among individuals and across schools calls for more local sensitivity in teaching policies. A common problem with state and federal policies is that reforms are frequently aimed across-the-board at entire classes of institutions and individuals. In order to be effective, policies aimed at improving the teaching profession and enabling teachers to have classroom careers need to recognize workplace and individual variation. For example, teachers argue that schools should be more professional environments. Yet what this means in terms of priorities for a school varies by context and current workplace conditions. For instance, a state or district mandate for discipline and order in the schools could improve teaching conditions at Roosevelt while inhibiting capacity for productive change at Brown.

The complexity of making schools better places to teach is exemplified by the existence of Brown's extensive system of time-compensated jobs (which gives certain teachers a reduced number of classes in exchange for taking up other responsibilities). This arrangement acts as a safety valve for many dedicated teachers who want to teach but find a full teaching load at an inner-city school overwhelming. The side effect of this system is the resentment of the majority of teachers because they are unable to take part in the limited number of these special positions and must carry the burden of full teaching loads and large classes. Maintaining this system may actually be counterproductive for the career attitudes of most of the faculty. Yet eliminating it would deprive many good teachers of needed relief. The best solution may be to expand the time-compensated positions so that all the teachers in this inner-city school could work with smaller or fewer classes. But this ideal solution requires sufficient financial resources, an assumption not easily defended during times of fiscal retrenchment. This example illustrates some of the complexities involved in devising solutions to the problem of retaining good teachers and points to the need for local elaboration and definition of reform policies.

The vignettes of some of the good teachers who left teaching warn against unintended and counterproductive effects of top-level reform efforts. Even schools with many enabling conditions for satisfying careers are vulnerable; state-level and district-level initiatives can still have a negative impact on teachers' careers. These experiences reinforce the argument for heightened sensitivity to local conditions and effects.

The experience of teachers interviewed also illustrates that career outcomes are affected by a configuration of many mutually reinforcing conditions in the workplace. Focusing on one aspect to the exclusion of the entire syndrome of institutional features will be ineffective.

Roosevelt High School, for instance, receives strong support for professional development workshops and in-services, an important component of a professional environment. But this feature alone is insufficient to ensure teachers' sense of efficacy and career commitment. The faculty frequently complains about the lack of support for discipline regarding student absences, the fragmented faculty relations, and the lack of faculty input at the district level.

Tinkering with only one or even two elements at the school would be insufficient, as these conditions independently and jointly contribute to job satisfaction. Policy strategies to address career and retention issues must take a systemic rather than piecemeal approach.

Bringing evaluation and staff development practices more in line with the career concerns raised here by teachers would contribute to such a systemic, integrated strategy. Isolated most of the day in their rooms, teachers — even low-involvement teachers — express the desire for concrete information about their effectiveness and suggestions for improvement. Although teachers are evaluated on a regular basis, they are rarely provided specific feedback on performance that would allow them to be reflective practitioners and to increase intrinsic rewards. For most administrators and teachers, evaluation is a ritualized activity that does little to promote improvement (McLaughlin & Pfeifer, 1988).

When a teacher does receive a negative evaluation, an adequate remediation system seldom exists. The chances for real change are slight, and teachers become stuck. The individual vignettes offer evidence that low involvement is an attitude constructed over the course of a career rather than a personal trait: Both good-fit and weak-fit teachers can become disengaged from teaching. This implies that teacher evaluation should be viewed as an integral part of long range, preventative strategies for the socialization and continuing professional growth of all teachers. Administratively, this involves workplace arrangements that provide rich opportunities for feedback and support from administrators and colleagues.

The potential use of teacher evaluation as an inducement for teachers to contribute their talents and efforts is not presently being realized. If evaluation is organized to support improvement and success in the classroom, rather than as a bureaucratic control mechanism to scrutinize teachers' practice or to rout out incompetents, it will represent an important source of intrinsic rewards. Such support is particularly critical for beginning teachers.

Staff development strategies, properly conceived, hold great promise for creating schools that support teachers who want to teach. Generally, however, staff development efforts are one-shot, short-term activities and thus fail to provide the kind of ongoing competence building that teachers say they want and need in order to have satisfying careers in the classroom.

The individual career stories also reveal that different incentives appeal to different individuals during different career stages. While new teachers value formal sources of training and feedback, veteran teachers stress the importance of more nontraditional and informal sources of growth: working together with colleagues, taking part in decisions, having special training opportunities outside the school, or taking on responsibilities in addition to teaching. Thus professional learning is more broadly conceived by teachers than by most administrators and staff development planners.

Ultimately, we must direct attention back to school conditions that support a sense of efficacy and competence. In teaching, just as in other professions dependent on employees' initiative, creativity, and self-directed behavior, motivation for performance cannot be mandated from above through traditional control and reward systems (Staw, 1983). In these occupations, administrative strategies should aim to support intrinsic needs and interests of employees; and the role of administrators should be viewed as facilitating opportunities for professional success, rather than as controlling work processes and employees.

The management of teachers' careers — in the sense of both retention and professional involvement — calls for a perspective on careers as a process of professional bonding and commitment. This process, beginning with a teacher's induction into the profession, requires nurturing through administrative and collegial support of teaching conditions and competence. A comprehensive career development approach, then, is essentially a strategy for continuous professional success.

Appendixes

References

Index

About the Author

Teacher Interview Questions

Teacher code #____
School code #_____

Demographic information

1. Note gender: male____ female____
   Note ethnic background: white____ black____ Hispanic___ Asian___ other_____
   Note age: 20s____ 30s___ 40s____ 50s____
2. Please tell me what range your salary falls in:
   $10,000 to $15,000____
   $15,001 to $20,000____
   $20,001 to $25,000____
   $25,001 to $30,000____
   $35,001 to $40,000____
   over $40,000 _____
3. How many children do you have? ____ Ages?_____
   Are you: married_____ single/divorced____
   Spouse's occupation: _____

Professional Experience

1. How many years have you been teaching? _____
2. How many years have you been at this particular school? ____
   (Workload)
   What grades and classes do you teach?
   How many different preparations do you have each day?
   What is the average number of students in each class?
   Do the students differ much in terms of ability?
   About how much time each week do you spend on discipline problems?
   How much preparation time are you given each week?
3. Why did you decide to become a teacher? *(Initial Commitment)*
   When did it happen?
   Did you consider other careers?
   When you first started, how long did you think you would stay in teaching? Why?
4. *(First teaching experience)*
   Tell me about your first teaching job. *(not student teaching)*
   What kind of students did you have?
   What do you remember best about it? *(probe: positive or negative experience?)*
   What was the most difficult thing about that year?
   Did you have a chance to observe other teachers that year?
   How often did your supervisor observe you and give you feedback?

What was the nature of interaction with the rest of the faculty? With the parents?
At the end of the first year, how did you feel about your success in teaching?
How did your supervisor evaluate your performance?

Career Commitment and Fit between Job and Individual

1. How does teaching fit what you want in a job? How does it not?
2. What do you see yourself doing in five years? *(In teaching or outside of teaching)*
   Why? Please rank the reasons you gave in the order of importance to you.

   For those who will leave teaching:
   At what point in your teaching career did you come to this decision? What were
   the circumstances?
   What conditions would cause you to change your mind?
   What would you look for in another job?

   For those who plan on staying in teaching:
   Can you remember when you decided that teaching was a career for you? What
   were the circumstances *(in your life and school)*?
   Have you ever considered leaving teaching before?
   How serious was the consideration?
   When and what were the circumstances for the consideration?
   What made you decide to stay after all?
   Under what conditions would you leave teaching?

   For those who are uncertain what they will do in five years:
   Have you ever seriously considered leaving teaching before?
   When and what were the circumstances for the consideration?
   What factors are the most important in your staying? Under what conditions
   would you leave teaching?
   What would you look for in another job?
   How easy do you think it would be for you to get another job that you like at this
   point in time? *(job alternatives)*
   What person or people at school or in your personal life have been most
   influential in your decision or attitude toward teaching as a career? *(social
   context)* In what way and how?

Professional Involvement

1. Thinking of your career as a whole, when have you felt your most effective as a
   teacher? Describe the circumstances surrounding that time.
2. How does your instructional effectiveness this past year or so compare with that
   period? Why?
   Most teachers have times or periods when they feel they are not as effective as
   they'd like to be. Tell me about one of those times and the circumstances
   surrounding it.
3. What kind of feedback has your principal or supervisor given you about your
   work as a teacher? *(Probe for quality or how it was helpful)*
4. What kind of professional development activities are most helpful to you?

Has the number of professional development activities that you participate in increased or decreased or remained about the same over the years? About how many do you participate in each year?

5. On an average how many hours a week outside of the normal school day do you spend on school-related matters, e.g., preparation, seeing students, and correcting papers?

6. How would the time and effort that you put into teaching compare with that of other teachers at your school?

7. As a teacher, what do you think is the most important factor in motivating students to learn? *(locus of control)*

Workplace Conditions

1. What school factors help you to do your best as a teacher?

2. How would you characterize the social relations among faculty at the school? Please give examples.

3. What kind of opportunities for professional development are offered by the school and the district? How often? How adequate are the offerings? How often do you participate?

4. What role do parents play in helping you do your job as a teacher?

5. How would you evaluate this school as a workplace?

TEACHERS WHO HAVE LEFT THE PROFESSION

In addition to questions asked of teachers still remaining in the profession:

When did you leave teaching?

What were the circumstances surrounding your decision?

Were you working at another job when you decided to leave?

What would have been necessary to keep you in teaching?

Did you already secure your next job when you left?

What kind of work are you doing now?

How satisfied are you with your work?

How does your salary now compare with your salary as a teacher?

How will your salary five to ten years from now compare with what you would be making in teaching?

Under what conditions would you consider going back to teaching?

Who was most influential in your decision to leave teaching? How did they influence you?

Would you rank your reasons for leaving in order of importance to you?

How would you evaluate your relative effectiveness to other teachers at your last school?

Teacher Career Commitment Survey

Please give me some background information and some information on your teaching assignment last semester. (Fill in the blanks.)

1a. How many years have you been teaching? _____years

1b. How many years have you been teaching at this school?_____

1c. How many years total have you taken a leave of absence or sabbatical from teaching? _____

1d. What department did you primarily teach in last semester? _____

1e. Number of periods each day that you taught last semester? _____periods

1f. Average class size? _____students

1g. Number of honors, advanced placement, or college preparatory classes that you taught last semester? _____

1h. Number of classes last semester with predominantly limited English speaking students or with students who are 3 years below grade level in reading or math? _____classes

2. Last semester, about what percentage of your time was spent handling classroom behavior or attendance problems? (Please check one.)

    _____ 0%-20%

    _____21%-40%

    _____41%-60%

    _____61%-80%

    _____81%-100%

3. Considering the number and kind of students and classes that you had to teach, how would you assess your workload last semester? (Circle a number.)

    very unmanageable 1 2 3 4 5 6 7 very manageable

4. Please check your employment status:

    _____substitute position

    _____temporary contract

    _____probationary status

    _____permanent or tenure position

5. In an average week, how many hours did you spend, in total, on school-related responsibilities—including the time you spent in the classroom, after school, and at home? _____ hours a week

6. Teachers often say that their success is due in part to their assignment. What percentage of the students did you feel you had accomplished your instructional goals with last semester? (Check one.)

    ____0%-20%

    ____21%-40%

    ____41%-60%

____61%-80%
____81%-100%

7. How effective did you feel you were in getting students to learn last year? (Circle a number.)

    very unsuccessful 1 2 3 4 5 6 7 very successful

The following questions ask more generally about your teaching career and your early years in the profession.

8. Why did you decide to become a teacher? (Please RANK your top THREE answers. Put a "1" next to your first choice, a "2" next to your second choice, and a "3" next to your third choice.)

    _____I fell into doing it by accident.
    _____I always wanted to or always thought I'd be good at it.
    _____I liked the vacations, work hours, or job security.
    _____I liked working with young people.
    _____I wanted to contribute to society/be of service to others.
    _____I was inspired or encouraged by my former teachers.
    _____My relatives were teachers.
    _____There were few other job opportunities when I decided to teach.
    _____I got a draft deferment.
    _____Other reason:_____

9. When you first started teaching, how long did you intend to stay in teaching? (Check one.)

    _____until retirement
    _____for a long time
    _____for a few years only
    _____until I had children
    _____I can't remember/I'm not sure

10. At the end of your first year of full-time teaching, how did you feel about your success as a teacher? (Circle a number.)

    very dissatisfied 1 2 3 4 5 6 7 very satisfied

11. In my teaching career, I have taken on the following positions or responsibilities: (Check ones applicable.)

    _____resource teacher
    _____curriculum developer
    _____counselor
    _____mentor teacher or trainer of teachers
    _____department chair
    _____program administrator at school site
    _____union representative/ negotiator
    _____principal/ assistant principal
    _____district-level administration

12. During your teaching career, how often did you work at another job during the school year for pay? (Check one.)

    _____Usually worked a second job

_____Sometimes worked a second job

_____Never worked a second job

13. Has the number of professional development activities that you participate in: (Check one.)

    _____decreased over the years?

    _____remained about the same?

    _____increased over the years?

Now I'd like to ask about your future work plans.

14. What is the likelihood of your being *in public school teaching* in five years? (Check the appropriate response.)

    _____highly likely

    _____somewhat likely

    _____uncertain

    _____somewhat unlikely

    _____highly unlikely

15. *If you intend to stay in the field of education* in the next five years, how likely is it that you will apply for the following positions? (Circle a number after EACH position.)

	very unlikely	somewhat unlikely	don't know	somewhat likely	very likely
a. Counselor	1	2	3	4	5
b. Resource teacher	1	2	3	4	5
c. Curriculum developer	1	2	3	4	5
d. Mentor teacher/trainer	1	2	3	4	5
e. Department chair	1	2	3	4	5
f. Dean	1	2	3	4	5
g. Union negotiator/representative	1	2	3	4	5
h. Principal/assistant principal	1	2	3	4	5
i. District-level administration	1	2	3	4	5

16. Please rate *each* of the following reasons in terms of its importance to your *staying in teaching*. Circle a number for each. Scale:

        1 = very unimportant

        2 = somewhat unimportant

        3 = neither important nor unimportant

        4 = somewhat important

        5 = very important

    a. 1 2 3 4 5   Collegial relations and interaction

    b. 1 2 3 4 5   Pay

    c. 1 2 3 4 5   Job security considerations

    d. 1 2 3 4 5   Promotion opportunities

    e. 1 2 3 4 5   Opportunities for professional development activities and stimulation

    f. 1 2 3 4 5   Recognition by peers/students

    g. 1 2 3 4 5   Relationship with supervisor

   h. 1 2 3 4 5 Satisfaction of work with students; seeing results of efforts
   i. 1 2 3 4 5 Location of school
   j. 1 2 3 4 5 Family considerations and responsibilities
 ˙ k. 1 2 3 4 5 Limited job opportunities outside of teaching
   1. 1 2 3 4 5 Schedule (hours, vacations)
   m. 1 2 3 4 5 Opportunity to pursue outside interests
   n. 1 2 3 4 5 Other (please specify):_____

17. Each reason in question #16 was labelled by a letter of the alphabet. Fill in the
    blanks below with the appropriate letter.
    My primary reason for staying in teaching:_____
    My second reason for staying in teaching:_____
    My third reason for staying in teaching:_____

18. Please rate EACH of the following reasons in terms of its importance to your
    LEAVING teaching. Circle the appropriate number for each reason:

                    1 = very unimportant
                    2 = somewhat unimportant
                    3 = neither important nor unimportant
                    4 = somewhat important
                    5 = very important

   a. 1 2 3 4 5 Job security considerations
   b. 1 2 3 4 5 Lack of promotion opportunities
   c. 1 2 3 4 5 Lack of opportunities for professional development and
                 stimulation
   d. 1 2 3 4 5 Poor collegial relations and interaction
   e. 1 2 3 4 5 Long hours
   f. 1 2 3 4 5 Lack of recognition/appreciation
   g. 1 2 3 4 5 Relationship with supervisor
   h. 1 2 3 4 5 Lack of sense of accomplishment with students
   i. 1 2 3 4 5 Family considerations and responsibilities
   j. 1 2 3 4 5 Pay
   k. 1 2 3 4 5 Poor student motivation or attendance
   1. 1 2 3 4 5 Monotony/routine of job
   m. 1 2 3 4 5 Health reasons
   n. 1 2 3 4 5 Low status of teaching
   o. 1 2 3 4 5 Other (please specify):_____

19. In question #18 above, each of the reasons was labelled by a letter of the alphabet.
    Fill in the following blanks with the appropriate letter.
    My primary reason for leaving teaching is:_____
    My second reason for leaving teaching is:_____
    My third reason for leaving teaching is:_____

20. *If there is some possibility of your leaving public school teaching* in five years,
    what do you anticipate doing instead?
    _____Retiring
    _____Raising children/spending time with my family
    _____Going back to school
    _____Teaching at the college level

_____Teaching in a private school
_____Getting another job outside of teaching
_____Going into school administration
_____I'm not sure.

21. Are you actively seeking or preparing yourself for another job outside of public high school teaching? (Check one.) _____yes _____no
22. Have you seriously considered leaving teaching in the past? _____yes _____no
23. During what year or years of your teaching career, did you seriously consider leaving? (e.g., 5th year of teaching) _____
24. Most teachers recall high points in their careers. As you think back on your teaching career, what year or years would you say you were your most effective with students? (e.g., from my 5th year to 7th year of teaching)
    from my _____year to my _____year of teaching
25. How would your principal or person in charge of evaluation rate your instructional effectiveness in the past year? (Circle a number.)
    below average 1 2 3 4 5 6 7 above average

Now I'd like to ask your opinion about various aspects of your teaching environment.

26. How would you assess the opportunities for professional growth and learning at your school? (Circle a number.)
    very inadequate 1 2 3 4 5 6 7 outstanding
27. How adequate is the following at your school: (Circle a number for each category.)
    a. materials   poor 1 2 3 4 5 6 7 excellent
    b. support for discipline poor 1 2 3 4 5 6 7 excellent
    c. parent support   poor 1 2 3 4 5 6 7 excellent
28. How satisfied are you with *teaching at this particular school*? (Circle a number.)
    very dissatisfied 1 2 3 4 5 6 7 very satisfied
29. How satisfied are you with *teaching as a job*? (Circle a number.)
    very dissatisfied 1 2 3 4 5 6 7 very satisfied
30. When you think of fellow teachers with whom you spend the most time, how would you characterize their satisfaction with teaching? (Circle a number.)
    very dissatisfied 1 2 3 4 5 6 7 very satisfied
31. Of the faculty with whom you have the most contact or know well, how would you characterize their effectiveness in teaching?
    very ineffective 1 2 3 4 5 6 7 very effective
32. Almost everyone experiences some stress in their lives, but some have a great deal of stress. How often did you feel under *great* stress last year? (Check one.)
    _____almost every day
    _____several days a week
    _____once or twice a week
    _____less often than once a week
    _____never
    _____not sure

33. How often do you wake up in the morning feeling glad to come to work? (Check one.)
    _____almost every day
    _____several days a week
    _____once or twice a week
    _____less often than once a week
    _____never
    _____not sure

34. Please rank the top *three* sources of stress in teaching for you. (Put a "1" next to the largest source, a "2" next to second largest, etc.)
    ____class size
    ____relations with supervisor
    ____discipline problems
    ____paperwork—correcting papers
    ____wide diversity of student academic needs and cultural backgrounds
    ____bureaucratic forms, reports
    ____lack of time
    ____lack of materials
    ____relations with colleagues
    ____other (please specify) _____

Now I'd like to ask a few questions which will help me understand some of your beliefs about teaching.

35. "When it comes right down to it, a teacher really can't do much because most of a student's motivation and performance depends on his or her home environment." Do you agree or disagree with this statement? Circle the appropriate number.
    strongly disagree 1 2 3 4 5 6 7 strongly agree

36. "If I really try hard, I can get through to even the most difficult or unmotivated students." Do you agree or disagree with this statement? Circle the appropriate number.
    strongly disagree 1 2 3 4 5 6 7 strongly agree

37. "I feel I am successful if I can really reach two or three students in each class." Do you agree or disagree with this statement? Circle the appropriate number.
    strongly disagree 1 2 3 4 5 6 7 strongly agree

Finally, I'd like to ask a series of personal background questions which will help me to establish a basis of comparison with other groups of teachers as well as to understand how issues and concerns may change as teachers become older.

38. Please check the appropriate category.
    a. Gender: _____male; _____female.
    b. Age: _____20-25 years old
            _____26-30
            _____31-35
            _____36-40
            _____41-45
            _____46-50

_____51-55

_____over 56 years old

   c. Check the highest degree you have received:

_____B.A. or B.S.

_____M.A., M.A.T., or M.S.

_____Ph.D. or Ed.D.

39. Please check your salary range (including stipends for extra duties, such as sports, clubs, mentor, department chair):

_____$10,000 to $15,000

_____$15,001 to $20,000

_____$20,001 to $25,000

_____$25,001 to $30,000

_____$30,001 to $35,000

_____$35,001 to $40,000

_____$40,001 to $45,000

_____over $45,000.

40. Are you (check one): _____single? _____married? _____divorced?

41a. How many children do you have? (Fill in the number.)_____

41b. How many of children are still living at home with you? _____

42a. What is the educational level of your father? (Check one.)

_____Less than high school education

_____High school graduate

_____Some college education

_____Bachelor's degree

_____Master's degree or above

42b. What is the educational level of your spouse (if you are married)? (Check one.)

_____Less than high school education

_____High school graduate

_____Some college education

_____Bachelor's degree

_____Master's degree or above

43. Which of the following income categories describes your total 1985 household income from all sources before taxes? (Check one.)

_____below $15,000

_____$15,001 to $20,000

_____$20,001 to $30,000

_____$30,001 to $40,000

_____$40,001 to $50,000

_____over $50,000

44. Ethnic Background. (Please check the appropriate category.)

_____white; _____black; _____Hispanic; _____Asian; _____other.

45. Are you one of the teachers I interviewed in the spring of 1986? (Check one.)

_____yes _____no

OPTIONAL. Please write me a note if you feel I have not covered a factor which is critical to your leaving or staying in teaching. Many, many thanks for your time and cooperation.

Additional Roles and Career Outcomes

Correlations from Survey Data

	Career Outcomes	
Additional Role	Sense of Success (*N* = 211)	Intention to Stay (*N* = 154)
Department Chair	.31**	.17*
Mentor Teacher	.14*	.13
Resource Teacher	.18**	.10
Curriculum Developer	.16*	.19**

** = significant at the .01 level

* = significant at the .05 level

Note: The number of respondents for Intentions to Stay is smaller than the number for Sense of Success because those intending to retire were excluded from the former calculation.

Sense of Success = What percentage of the students did you feel you had accomplished your instructional goals with last semester?

10	0-20%	(1)
30	21-40%	(2)
48	41-60%	(3)
75	61-80%	(4)
48	81-100%	(5)

Intention to Leave or Stay = What is the likelihood of your being in public school teaching in five years? (Check the appropriate response.)

18	Highly unlikely	(1)
9	Somewhat unlikely	(2)
27	Uncertain	(3)
15	Somewhat likely	(4)
85	Highly likely	(5)

References

Argyris, C. (1957). *Personality and organization.* New York: Harper.

Ashton, P. T., & Webb, R. B. (1986). *Making a difference: Teachers' sense of efficacy and student achievement.* New York: Longman.

Bacharach, S. M., Bauer, S. C., & Conley, S. C. (1986). Organizational analysis of stress: The case of secondary and elementary schools. *Journal of Work and Occupations, 13,* 7–32.

Ball, S. J., & Goodson, I. F. (1985). *Teachers' lives and careers.* Philadelphia: Falmer.

Barnard, C. I. (1962). *The functions of the executive* (rev. ed.). Cambridge, MA: Harvard University Press.

Becker, H. S., & Carper, J. (1966). Professional identification. In D. L. Mills & H. M. Vollmer (Eds.), *Professionalization* (pp. 101–109). Englewood Cliffs, NJ: Prentice-Hall.

Berlew, D. E., & Hall, D. T. (1977). The socialization of managers: Effects of expectations on performance. *Administrative Science Quarterly, 2,* 207–223.

Berman, P., & McLaughlin, M. (1978). *Federal programs supporting educational change* (Vol. 7). Santa Monica, CA: Rand Corporation.

Berry, B. (1985). *A case study of teacher attrition in a metropolitan school system in the Southeast.* Research Triangle Park, NC: Southeastern Regional Council for Educational Improvement.

Biklen, S. K. (1986). I have always worked: Elementary schoolteaching as a career. *Phi Delta Kappan, 67,* 404–412.

Bruno, J. E., & Doscher, M. L. (1981). Contributing to the harms of racial isolation: Analysis of requests for teacher transfer in a large urban school district. *Educational Administration Quarterly, 17,* 93–103.

Chapman, D. (1984). Teacher retention: The test of a model. *American Educational Research Journal, 21,* 645–658.

Charters, W. W., Jr. (1965). The relation of morale to turnover among teachers. *American Education Research Journal, 2,* 163–173.

Charters, W. W., Jr. (1976). Some "obvious" facts about the teaching career. *Educational Administration Quarterly, 3,* 182–193.

Cox, H., & Wood, J. R. (1980). Organizational structure and professional alienation: The case of public school teachers. *Peabody Journal of Education, 58*(1), 1–6.

Darling-Hammond, L., Wise, A. E., & Pease, S. R. (1983). Teacher evaluation in the organizational context: A review of the literature. *Review of Educational Research, 53,* 285–328.

Deci, E. L. (1976). The hidden costs of rewards. *Organizational Dynamics, 4,* 61–72.

Dworkin, A. G. (1980). The changing demography of public school teachers: Some implications for faculty turnover in urban areas. *Sociology of Education, 53,* 65–73.

Edelwich, J. (1980). *Burn-out: Stages of disillusionment in the helping professions.* New York: Human Sciences Press.

Educational Research Service, Inc. (1985). *Educator opinion poll.* Arlington, VA: Author.

Etzioni, A. (1969). *The semi-professions and their organizations.* New York: Free Press.

Freiberg, H. J. (1984, December). Master teacher programs: Lessons from the past. *Educational Leadership,* pp. 16–21.

Geer, B. (1966). Occupational commitment and the teaching profession. *The School Review, 74*(1), 221–234.

Hackman, J. R., & Oldham, G. R. (1980). *Work redesign.* Reading, MA: Addison-Wesley.

Hall, D. T., & Schneider, B. (1973). *Organizational climates and careers: The work lives of priests.* New York: Seminar Press.

Hallinger, P., & Murphy, J. F. (1986). The social context of effective schools. *American Journal of Education, 94,* 328–355.

Harris, Louis, & Associates. (1985). *The American teacher 1985.* New York: Metropolitan Life Insurance Co.

Hawley, W. D., & Rosenholtz, S. J. (1984). Good schools: What research says about improving student achievement. *Peabody Journal of Education, 61*(4), 1–178.

Herriott, R. E., & St. John, N. (1966). *Social class and the urban school.* New York: Wiley.

Heyns, B. (1988). Educational defectors: A first look at teacher attrition in the NLS-72. *Educational Researcher, 17,* 24–31.

Hughes, E. C. (1937). Institutional office and the person. *American Journal of Sociology, 43,* 404–413.

Johnson, S. M. (1986). Incentives for teachers: What motivates, what matters. *Educational Administration Quarterly, 22,* 54–79.

Kanter, R. M. (1983). *The change masters.* New York: Simon & Schuster.

Karasek, R. A. (1979). Job demands, job decision latitude, and mental strain: Implications for job redesign. *Administrative Science Quarterly, 24,* 285–308.

Katz, R. (1982). *Career issues in human resource management.* Englewood Cliffs, NJ: Prentice-Hall.

Little, J. W. (1982). Norms of collegiality and experimentation: Workplace conditions of school success. *American Educational Research Journal, 19,* 325–340.

Locke, E. A. (1976). The nature and causes of job satisfaction. In M. D.

Dunnette (Ed.), *Handbook of industrial and organizational psychology* (pp. 1297–1349). Chicago: Rand McNally.

Lortie, D. C. (1975). *Schoolteacher: A sociological study.* Chicago: University of Chicago Press.

Louis, M. R. (1980). Toward an understanding of career transitions. In C. B. Derr (Ed.), *Work, family, and the career* (pp. 200–218). New York: Praeger.

Macrorie, K. (1984). *Twenty teachers.* New York: Oxford University Press.

March, J. G., & Simon, H. A. (1958). *Organizations.* New York: Wiley.

Mason, W. S., Dressel, R. J., & Bain, R. K. (1959). Sex role and career orientations of beginning teachers. *Harvard Educational Review, 29,* 370–383.

McLaughlin, M. W., & Marsh, D. D. (1978). Staff development and school change. *Teachers College Record, 80*(1), 69–94.

McLaughlin, M. W., & Pfeifer, R. S. (1988). *Teacher evaluation: Improvement, accountability, and effective learning.* New York: Teachers College Press.

McLaughlin, M. W., Pfeifer, R. S., Swanson-Owens, D., & Yee, S. (1986). Why teachers won't teach. *Phi Delta Kappan, 67,* 420–425.

McLaughlin, M. W., & Yee, S. M. (1988). School as a place to have a career. In A. Lieberman (Ed.), *Building a professional culture in schools* (pp. 23–45). New York: Teachers College Press.

McNeil, L. (1986). *Contradictions of control: School structure and school knowledge.* New York: Routledge & Kegan Paul.

Metz, M. H. (1986). *Different by design: The context and character of three magnet schools.* London: Routledge & Kegan Paul.

Metz, M. H. (1988, April). *Teachers' ultimate dependence on their students: Implications for teachers' responses to student bodies of differing social class.* Paper presented at the annual meeting of the American Educational Research Association, New Orleans, LA.

Mobley, W. H. (1982). *Employee turnover: Causes, consequences, and control.* Reading, MA: Addison-Wesley.

Mowday, R. T., Porter, L. W., & Steers, R. M. (1982). *Employee-organization linkages: The psychology of commitment, absenteeism and turnover.* New York: Academic Press.

National Education Association (1987). *Status of the American public school teacher, 1985–86.* West Haven, CT: Author.

Newman, F. M., Rutter, R. A., & Smith, M. S. (1985). *Exploratory analysis of high school teacher climate* (Grant No. NIE-G-84-0008). Madison, WI: Wisconsin Center for Education Research.

Nias, J. (1985). Reference groups in primary teaching: Talking, listening, and identity. In S. Ball & I. Goodson (Eds.), *Teachers' lives and careers* (pp. 105–119). Philadelphia: Falmer.

Purkey, S. C., & Smith, M. S. (1983). Effective schools — A review. *Elementary School Journal, 83,* 427–452.

Ritzer, G. (1977). *Working: Conflict and change.* Englewood Cliffs, NJ: Prentice-Hall.

Schein, E. (1977). Organizational socialization and the profession of management. In B. Staw (Ed.), *Psychological foundation of organizational behavior* (pp. 210–224). Santa Monica, CA: Goodyear.

Schein, E. (1978). *Career dynamics: Matching individual and organizational needs.* Reading, MA: Addison-Wesley.

Schlechty, P. C., & Vance, V. S. (1981). Do academically able teachers leave education? The North Carolina case. *Phi Delta Kappan, 63,* 106–113.

Schlechty, P. C., & Vance, V. S. (1983). Recruitment, selection and retention: The shape of the teaching force. *Elementary School Journal, 83,* 469–487.

Scott, W. R. (1966). Professionals in bureaucracies — Areas of conflict. In H. Vollmer & D. Mills (Eds.), *Professionalization* (pp. 265–274). Englewood Cliffs, NJ: Prentice-Hall.

Scott, W. R. (1981). *Organizations: Rational, natural, and open systems.* Englewood Cliffs, NJ: Prentice-Hall.

Shedd, J. B. (1987). *Involving teachers in school and district decision making: A review of research and summary of issues.* Ithaca, NY: Organizational Analysis and Practice.

Sikes, P. (1985). The life cycle of the teacher. In S. Ball & I. Goodson (Eds.), *Teachers' lives and careers* (pp. 27–60). Philadelphia: Falmer.

Simon, H. A. (1961). *Administrative behavior.* New York: Macmillan.

Slocum, W. L. (1966). *Occupational careers: A sociological perspective.* Chicago: Aldine.

Spuck, D. W. (1974). Reward structures in the public high school. *Educational Administration Quarterly, 10,* 18–34.

Staw, B. (1983, Summer). Motivation research versus the art of faculty management. *Review of Higher Education,* pp. 301–321.

Stebbins, R. A. (1970). Career: the subjective approach. *Sociological Quarterly, 11,* 32–49.

Talbert, J. E. (1986). The staging of teachers' careers: An institutional perspective. *Work and Occupations, 13,* 421–443.

Unruh, W. R. (1979). Career decision making: Theory construction and evaluation. In A. M. Mitchell, G. B. Jones, & J. D. Krumboltz (Eds.), *Social learning and career decision making* (pp. 5–18). Cranston, RI: Carroll Press.

Van Maanen, J. (Ed.). (1977). *Organizational careers: Some new perspectives.* New York: Wiley.

Van Maanen, J., & Barley, S. R. (1984). Occupational communities: Culture and control in organizations. In B. M. Staw (Ed.), *Research in organizational behavior* (Vol. 6, pp. 287–365). Greenwich, CT: JAI Press.

Wanous, J. P. (1980). *Organizational entry: Recruitment, selection, and socialization of newcomers.* Reading, MA: Addison-Wesley.

Yee, S. M. (1986, April). *Teaching as a career: Promotion versus development.* Paper presented at the annual meeting of the American Educational Research Association, San Francisco, CA.

Index

About the Author

Sylvia Mei-ling Yee is a program executive at the San Francisco Foundation, where she is responsible for grantmaking in education and community health and specializes in children and youth issues. She began her career in education as a high school social studies teacher in the early 1970s, after receiving her B.A. from Stanford University and an M.A.T. from Reed College. Her interest in minority and urban education issues eventually led her to administrative positions in programs serving inner-city students in San Francisco, first at the elementary level and later at a state university. After a three-year sojourn in the People's Republic of China, where she was a lecturer in English at Wuhan University, she returned to Stanford University and began graduate studies in the School of Education, specializing in organizational analysis, evaluation, and school reform. She received her Ph.D. in Administration and Policy Analysis in 1988.